Upstaters

Upstaters

Poets, Pols, Prophets, and Bush-League Heroes of Upstate New York

BILL KAUFFMAN

excelsior editions

Cover photos taken by Mike Janes, Sandra Kauffman, Lucine Kauffman, and Bill Kauffman.

Published by State University of New York Press, Albany

Printed in the United States of America

EU GPSR Authorised Representative:
Logos Europe, 9 rue Nicolas Poussin, 17000, La Rochelle, France
contact@logoseurope.eu

Excelsior Editions is an imprint of State University of New York Press

For information, contact State University of New York Press, Albany, NY
www.sunypress.edu

Library of Congress Cataloging-in-Publication Data

Name: Kauffman, Bill, 1959– author.
Title: Upstaters : poets, pols, prophets, and bush-league heroes of Upstate New York / Bill Kauffman.
Description: Albany : State University of New York Press, [2026]. | Series: Excelsior editions | Includes bibliographical references and index.
Identifiers: LCCN 2026006287 | ISBN 9798855808551 (pbk. : alk. paper) | ISBN 9798855808568 (epub) | ISBN 9798855808575 (PDF)
Subjects: LCSH: Upstate New York (N.Y.)—Social life and customs. | Upstate New York (N.Y.)—History. | LCGFT: Biographies.
Classification: LCC F126.8 .K38 2026
LC record available at https://lccn.loc.gov/2026006287

For Mom and Dad, with love and gratitude

Upstate is a country.

—Carl Carmer

Now, brooding thro' a history of the early church,
I identify with everybody, even the heresiarchs

—John Berryman, "Eleven Addresses to the Lord"

Contents

Places

Acknowledgments

Profuse thanks to the Richards, Kostelanetz and Carlin, and to the editors who commissioned many tiles of this mosaic: Tom Bissell, George Hodgman, David Congdon, Peter Mommsen, Shana Goodwin, Karl Zinsmeister, Freddy Gray, Dominic Green, Oliver Wiseman, Teresa Mull, Zach Christenson, Wendell Tripp, Jason Peters, Barbara Tipton, Chilton Williamson, Russ Salway, Martha Treichler, Bill Treichler, Kenneth Turan, Dan McCarthy, Bob Merry, Jim Antle, and Johnny Burtka. I'm also grateful to Diane Ganeles, the excellent production editor (and Buffalo Bills fan), and to our daughter and son-in-law, Gretel Kauffman-Dee and Mark Dee, for their heroic indexing—with Scooter's assistance.

Permissions/Thanks

"Barber B. Conable Jr.: Our Statesman" is taken from Bill Kauffman, ed., *The Congressional Journal of Barber B. Conable, Jr., 1968–1984* (University Press of Kansas, 2021), xvii–xxvii, reprinted with permission of the University Press of Kansas.

Portions of "Henry W. Clune Knew His Place" and "John Gardner: This Bud's for Us" appeared in *Dispatches from the Muckdog Gazette: A Mostly Affectionate Account of a Small Town's Fight to Survive*, published in 2003 by Henry Holt.

Introduction

When in 1988 my wife, Lucine, and I repatriated to my hometown of Batavia, New York, I had the romantic and probably ridiculous notion that I was going to reignite the fires that had long since faded to ashes and embers in the Burned-Over District, as historians call our history-haunted swath between Utica and Lake Erie, give or take the Queen City and the Southern Tier.

I was young, with a touch of late-twenties megalomania, and I was ablaze with the mad and naive enthusiasm of the revenant. Withal, I was under the spell of the long-forgotten Hamlin Garland's 1894 manifesto *Crumbling Idols*, wherein the Dakotan asserted, "Each locality must produce its own literary record" and prophesied a national literature built on a Whitmanian efflorescence of many voices, many accents, many localisms.

I am no longer young—unless your measuring stick is Henry W. Clune, the centenarian novelist of Rochester who is the subject of our first profile—but I am no less in love with my homeplace.

I wish you a love of your own with your place, wherever it may be, however newly arrived or deeply rooted you may be, for as Booker T. Washington wisely advised, we must cast down our buckets where we are.

Peace and love,
Bill Kauffman

PEOPLE: PORTRAITS

1

Henry W. Clune Knew His Place

2003

Why hasten on;—hast thou a fairer home?
Has God more richly blest the world than here,
That thou in haste would'st from thy country roam . . .

—Jones Very

Henry W. Clune and Bill Kauffman, three weeks before Henry's death. Photo by Lucine Kauffman.

I met Henry W. Clune in the fall of 1990, when he was 100 years old. I was writing a profile of him for the *Los Angeles Times Book Review.* He had just published his thirteenth book, a collection of short stories, and was grousing that his editor "could better use her ability to edit a seed catalogue." Henry had scotched plans by admirers for a fete on the occasion of his centenary because "they want you on display like the bearded woman in the Ringling Show or the two-headed calf on the carnival lot." (Anachronistic diction is the badge of the longevous. In *Retreat,* Henry's only unpublished novel, a sympathetic depiction of a homosexual Vietnam-era draft dodger and his befuddled middle-class family, an antiwar protester yells to his comrades, "Cheese it, the cops!")

Born in 1890, on the cusp of the Lost Generation, Henry W. Clune was older than Fitzgerald by six years and Hemingway by nine. For the better part of a century—from 1913 to 1969, with sabbaticals for Mr. Wilson's War and one or two other detours—he wrote "Seen and Heard," the most popular column in Frank Gannett's flagship, the Rochester *Democrat and Chronicle.*

In his spare and slack time he wrote six novels and seven books on regional subjects, including *The Genesee* in the Rivers of America series. "I am a provincial by instinct, by design, and by practice," Henry boasted. He stood *on* what he stood *for*: Clune lived in Rochester and the neighboring village of Scottsville for all but his few wanderlust years. For most of those decades Henry also resided in that most interesting of precincts, the outskirts of fame. In 1921, after a whirlwind courtship, he married Olympic swimmer Charlotte Boyle, daughter of rakish adventurer Joe "King of the Klondike" Boyle, who was the inamorato of Marie, Queen of Romania. The New York *World* immortalized the obscure swain Henry in "The Wooing of Charlotte Boyle" and then anathematized him in "The Shower that Shattered a Mermaid Friendship." (Just a couple of years earlier, Henry had ripped out a photograph of Miss Boyle—whom he had never met—from a magazine and pasted it in his scrapbook. He conspired with a friend to bring her to Rochester for a swimming exhibition; they married barely a month after their first meeting.)

Clune's early novels grazed the bottom of the bestseller lists, but luck deserted him at a couple of critical junctures. "I had a lot of near-misses," he sighed. "I'd be wearing diamonds if I had all the stuff they told me I'd have."

Henry's first novel, *The Good Die Poor* (1937), a picaresque tale of a scheming newspaperman, was purchased by Warner Brothers as a vehicle for Bette Davis and Edward G. Robinson—the thought of those two in a clinch defines detumescence—and never made.

His next novel, the prescient political satire *Monkey on a Stick* (1940), in which a platitudinous salesman with a flair for radio runs for president, was praised by Dawn Powell and the Communist *Daily Worker* but otherwise forgotten. When Frank Capra stole the plot for *Meet John Doe*, the resulting legal settlement was a windfall for the Clunes.

Henry's magnum opus was *By His Own Hand* (1952), in which Rochester's George Eastman is transmuted into Alan Wesley, a steel-willed industrialist who enriches a city and smashes its fusty social hierarchy. *By His Own Hand*—Henry had preferred the less ponderous "The Stars Have Monstrous Eyes" as a title—is one of the best American novels of the titanic businessman. (Wesley bears comparison to Dreiser's Frank Cowperwood.) It also inspired Clune to dreams of a fame that never came.

"When I signed the contract at the Grosvenor Hotel," he recalled, "George Brett, the president of Macmillan, said, 'Mr. Clune, if you'll sign this contract we believe we've got the most popular success since *Gone with the Wind*.' "

It didn't happen: Orville Prescott of *The New York Times* dismissed the book as "vulgar petty gossip" and though it was praised elsewhere and sold 55,000 copies, it fell far short of Brett's promise.

In best auctorial fashion, Henry bore Prescott a grudge unto the grave. "It was a hatchet job," he said, and he knew the reason why: "One minor character says she was bored with boys telling her about a Psi U house party at Williams. Mr. Prescott was a Psi U at Williams." On throwaway lines is our history written.

Fortune also frowned on Clune's fourth novel, *The Big Fella* (1956)—his own favorite—which charted the rise and fall of a rapscallion political boss modeled after Rochester's George W. Aldridge. When Clune's editor Cecil Scott was pushed to the margins with an eye infection, the book's publication was delayed three months. In the interim, Edwin O'Connor's *The Last Hurrah* appeared, and *The Big Fella* would disappear in the shadow of O'Connor's roistering hero Frank Skeffington.

After our first meeting, I returned almost weekly to Henry's home in Scottsville, where we sat in the fire-warmed den under signed photos of such forgotten novae as Gilda Gray (mentioned in *The Great Gatsby*!) and drank martinis mixed by his son Peter. In the early stages of our friendship I had assumed that each visit would be my last, but after a while, six months or so, I gave it no more thought, concluding, on the basis of all available evidence, that Henry would live forever.

No American writer has ever belonged to a place as Henry W. Clune (he was persnickety if one left out the *W*) belonged to gray Rochester.

His father once lived in the same boardinghouse as did Susan B. Anthony (who was no barrel of laughs, pa reported). His mother was one of twelve employees on George Eastman's first payroll. Henry's sense of rootedness was as profound as is humanly possible.

"I liked London . . . but it wasn't Rochester," Henry once wrote, seriously. He loved his city, wryly, and with a capaciousness that could take in dowager and race-track tout. He also possessed the sort of reactionary streak I love: he lamented the loss of "provincial ambiance" that Rochester's corporatization entailed, and in *The Genesee*, he cursed the "motorboats" that had "disturbed the placid waters of our river [and] befouled the air above it with their oily stench."

Henry lived almost all his life under the charm of the Genesee, which never passes through Genesee County, and along its metaphorical banks. A verse by the early-nineteenth-century poet William Hosmer, the bard of Avon, New York, seems apt.

Ambition from the scenes of youth
May others lure away
To chase the phantom of renown
Throughout their little day;
I would not, for a palace proud
And slave of pliant knee,
Forsake a cabin in thy vale,
My own dark Genesee.

Henry cheerfully conceded his parochialism. He loved quoting Bernard DeVoto: "Why see Paris, France, if you haven't seen Paris, Illinois?" And he had before him the cautionary examples of his Paris, France–seeing Rochester friends Philip Barry and Louise Brooks.

Philip Barry grew up several blocks from Henry's native Linden Street. An Irish-Catholic boy of considerable charm, Phil left the Flower City for Yale and later George Pierce Baker's drama workshop at Harvard (where Thomas Wolfe was a classmate). He never looked back.

"Phil was a dandy," Henry recalled. *Was he ever*. He married a rich girl, lived in Cannes and East Hampton, and wrote a series of clever drawing-room comedies that made him "a tidy sum of money," as Wolfe noted, not without envy.

Two of Barry's plays—*Holiday* and *The Philadelphia Story*—were delightfully filmed, but except for an anthology edited by Brendan Gill, the playwright rests in obscurity. "Phil is even forgotten in Rochester," Henry used to fret. Barry's sophisticated epigrams and horsey-set badinage are alien to his native soil and simply cannot survive without continuous sunlight from stars afar. Phil Barry didn't need a hometown, and in death, I'm afraid, his hometown doesn't need him.

Louise Brooks staggered into Rochester because she had nowhere else to go. She was a Kansas chorine who made a slew of silent movies, most famously the German G. W. Pabst's *Pandora's Box*, in which she played Lulu, the guileless hedonist, irresistible to men (among others), until, lucklessly, she picks up Jack the Ripper. (Talk about Mr. Goodbar!)

Louise was an erratic, arrogant, dissipated beauty. She slept with everyone except the moguls, and she detested Hollywood while taking its money. The industry was run, she later wrote, by "coarse exploiter[s] who propositioned every actress and policed every set. To love books was a big laugh. There was no theatre, no opera, no concerts—just those god-damned movies." A has-been at thirty-three, Louise fled the glitz.

She ended up back in Wichita, teaching dance, until a scandal involving the better part of a high school football team made it best for her to move on. She drifted downward until 1956, when she settled in Rochester at the invitation of the curator of the Eastman Museum of Photography, whose archives she mined to write the razor-sharp essays later compiled in *Lulu in Hollywood*.

Louise Brooks and Henry W. Clune began a fitful, exasperating friendship. She swam in gin on dinner dates, Henry remembered, but her bile was . . . bewitching. She lived in a dingy apartment on Goodman Street, paid for by William Paley, an old flame. Henry hated to stop by her tenement because "she'd never stop talking. You could never get out."

(I repeated this to our Washington DC friend Jay Pascucci, a Brooks fancier. He was aghast. "She was casting pearls before swine!" he exclaimed. I relayed this to Henry. "Swine," he grinned, "oh, that's great. I've been called worse"—not least by Louise, who frequently vilipended him as a "goddam bourgeois." Henry asked me to extend to Jay an open invitation to "stop by and hear all about Louise. I'll tell him she wasn't any great beauty. She reminded me of general housework.")

General housework? Cheese it: the cops!

Louise reentered the Celebrity Nation in 1979, thanks to Kenneth Tynan's lengthy paean in *The New Yorker*. European cineastes had long insisted, "There is no Garbo! There is no Dietrich! There is only Louise Brooks!" Finally, cisatlantic adulation was hers. She died in 1985; four years later, Knopf published Barry Paris's 609-page biography. "Mose," Henry growled, his saltiest epithet. "Six hundred pages for an actress? That movie *Pandora's Box* bored me to tears."

Henry showed me some poison-pen billets-doux he'd received from Louise in her last crippled years. Brooks soaked even her Christmas cards in vitriol: Under the stenciled "Season's Greetings" her chicken scratch lacerated Humphrey Bogart ("a gentleman and a bore") and Will Rogers (a stone-drunk whose companionship all avoided: "No wonder he never met a man he didn't like"). She even slagged the man who had resurrected her reputation. ("Tynan was no fag—just your usual upper-class English pervert.")

Louise refused to indulge Henry's provincialism. "I hated you," she reminisced fondly in one Christmas letter, typically devoid of Christian charity. Henry was too . . . "Rochester." She airily dismissed Clune's claim that his friend Phil Barry was the equal of O'Neill and Coward. She reviled Rochester as her Coventry. "To be a rebel is to court extinction," Louise once murmured in a self-dramatizing fog. For all her tartness and capricious debauchery and undeniable pulchritude, I wonder if she ever realized that Henry, doggedly and faithfully creating a Rochester literature of place, was more of a rebel than she ever dreamed of being.

"I've had a wonderful life," Henry often said, as he sat in his den, fire crackling, drinks poured, lights on high, urging me to read Marquand, read Macaulay, read Hemingway (the short stories). He was lucid till the end; a few days before his death at the age of 105, he called to urge me to "read Zola." A Francophobe, I still have not; sorry, Henry.

Three weeks before his death, I gave a talk at the Richmond Library on "The Life and Work of Henry W. Clune." Peter drove Henry to Batavia; Henry shuffled in, crouched over his cane, and sat in the front, probably hearing about half of what I said. He had often asked me to give the eulogy at his funeral. I thought of this as a dress rehearsal, with the guest of honor open-eyed. I was admiring, and sincerely so, in my talk. He was pleased.

Within a month I reworked the tenses and gave much the same talk at Christ Church Episcopal on Rochester's East Avenue. Standing in the same pulpit from which the bishop had once denounced the heretic Algernon Crapsey, I offered Carl Carmer's poem about an old farm couple.

Late June he died
"Don't mourn," said she,
"Things keep on
That folks don't see."

But Henry was something of an egotist, and I knew that he'd be peeved if I didn't quote from his own work. So I concluded my remarks with Henry's valediction from his penultimate book, a memoir:

"I have known no great triumphs. Flowers have not been flung in my path; I have heard no cries of 'Viva!' But I have done almost everything I wanted to do. In the vespertine quiet of a warm summer evening, on the terrace in front of our house, I have occasionally heard a whispered query: Where would you rather be than here? The answer is prompt and inevitable. Nowhere else in the world. Except for a couple of departures in early manhood in futile quest of greener pastures, I have lived all my long life no more than fifteen miles from the place of my birth; thirty-seven years in the city of Rochester, fifty-five years in the same house with the same wife in the village of Scottsville. I always had a lurking wish to appear considerable in my native place, and in a career of nearly three-score years in the newspaper business in Rochester I achieved status and a desirable prestige. I always liked it here."

And "here" always liked Henry.

2

Walter D. Edmonds

Our Stalwart, 1992

Walter D. Edmonds. Collection of Bill Kauffman.

In December 1991, I drove along Governor Dewey's dubious legacy, the New York State Thruway, to visit Upstate's biographer, novelist Walter D. Edmonds. Mr. Edmonds lives in Concord, Massachusetts, Valhalla of American writers. His circa 1870 home and garden stand along the banks of Thoreau's river and not far from the hillock in Sleepy Hollow Cemetery in which repose the families of Emerson, Thoreau, Hawthorne, and Edmonds's ancestors, the Alcotts. This is a curious place for Edmonds. He has roots in ghostly Concord, but the plain folk of his novels are far removed from fey Transcendentalists and earnest reformers. One shudders to imagine Chad Hanna running into Bronson Alcott.

Mr. Edmonds is courtly and eighty-eight (at the time of our meeting); his accent, fittingly, is a hybrid of high Brahmin and Oneida County hick. He has wrapped an old flannel shirt around his button-down and tie; his cat, Poupette, ambles over couch and table and tape recorder and guest with feline insouciance.

Walter Dumaux Edmonds was born in 1903 to the central New York aristocracy. His father practiced law in New York City, so the boy early on understood that New York is two—at least two—different states. ("Upstate is a country," as Carl Carmer, the Oak Orchard–bred folklorist, used to say.) He speaks with obvious pride of his birth—on the farm in Boonville rather than in Babylon on the Hudson—and he says that Edmund Wilson envied him his local nativity. One of the news clips he is proudest of is from the *Boonville Herald*: "Boonville Boy Writes Book."

(What is it about Utica? Although it is Upstate New York's eighth largest city, its environs nurtured three of our finest literary men: Edmonds, Harold Frederic, and Edmund Wilson. Not to mention New York's two greatest political personages of their day—Horatio Seymour and Roscoe Conkling.)

From the first, Edmonds was enchanted by life in the Black River country. "I was much closer to the farm life than I was to the family life, and much more at home in the farmhouses," he says. The Black River Canal, a feeder to the Erie, was "right within view of our back porch. You couldn't see the boats, but you could see the steersmen and the mules or horses. It was about three-fourths of a mile, and I regret to say that we used to throw tomatoes at them. They'd done nothing to us—it was sheer vandalism—but we knew they couldn't pursue us for any length of time."

This son of an estivating laird was filled with curiosity about the lives of the local people. He recalls one eventful stay in Boonville: "I spent a winter on the farm. Father thought it would be good for my health and he made me promise to be outside every day for at least three hours. Most of the time I would snowshoe up and down the river. I had a good many friends up and down the river and I'd spend time with them. Most of the material [for *Rome Haul*] came out of things they told me. Also, in the farmhouse that winter I found two scrapbooks my grandfather in Utica had kept from before father's birth in 1850. A lot of them had to do with happenings on the canal. That's where I got the reference to the canal agency for bachelor boaters. Supplying girls—I don't know what that would be today!"

At Harvard, young Edmonds began writing about life along the canal. An early story, "The End of the Tow-Path," caught the eye of Professor Charles Townsend Copeland, who helped him sell it to Scribner's. "It was the only story I wrote in longhand," remembers Edmonds. "[Copeland] said, 'You take it back and get it typed and I'll send it down to Max Perkins at Scribner's.' That was the opening of my junior year but they didn't publish it till I graduated. I was very cross about that."

Rome Haul appeared shortly thereafter, in 1929, and for the next two decades Walter Edmonds established himself as the most significant Upstate novelist since Harold Frederic. His early novels sold well and received friendly notices; his short stories, some of which were collected in *Mostly Canallers* (1934), appeared in such magazines as *The Atlantic Monthly* and the *Saturday Evening Post*. *Drums Along the Mohawk* (1936) was kept from a lengthy stay atop the bestseller lists only by the contemporaneous issue of Margaret Mitchell's *Gone with the Wind*. (Edmonds's original title, *The Starving Wilderness*, was scrapped because "in the Depression that wasn't a happy title at all.")

Edmonds recalls the writing of *Drums*: "I read [Harold Frederic's] *In the Valley* and that was an influence. I was thinking about it as I wrote *Drums Along the Mohawk*. I had a terrible time getting *Drums Along the Mohawk* started. I worked at it for over a year and I had 800–900 pages of manuscript stacked up. . . . [It] became a children's book called *Wilderness Clearing*. But then I finally hit on the beginning that I have. It's not a terribly good beginning: it's serviceable. . . . I [started] in July of 1935 . . . and I finished it on New Year's Eve."

Frederic was an influence, but Upstate's other eminent American novelist was not. "I thought [James Fenimore Cooper] was perfectly ridiculous," chuckles Edmonds. "I remember mother reading all of Fenimore Cooper and I was fascinated but I said this is nonsense. Nobody could see a nail at 400 yards: even if he could hit it, he just wouldn't see it! I know just what happened. He came back from England to his father's planned development in Cooperstown and he threw his weight around as the squire and then he got around, asking about things in the woods, and I can just see the old-timers telling him ridiculous things and he swallowed the whole works and they came out in his book."

Hollywood filmed *Drums Along the Mohawk*, as well as *Chad Hanna* and *Rome Haul* (twice), which had been adapted by Marc Connelly and Frank B. Elser as *The Farmer Takes a Wife*. "I didn't like it very much," says Edmonds of *Drums*, one of director John Ford's few botches. The pampered French poodle Claudette Colbert was badly miscast as a frontier wife, although Henry Fonda made a fine Gil Martin. (Fonda, whose family name graces a town in Montgomery County, appeared in film versions of all three Edmonds novels. His first big break came on stage in *The Farmer Takes a Wife*. *Drums Along the Mohawk*, sandwiched between the extraordinary Ford–Fonda collaborations *Young Mr. Lincoln* and *The Grapes of Wrath*, secured Fonda's burgeoning reputation as the apotheosis of the "good old American type.")

Beginning in the 1940s, Walter Edmonds wrote a series of books for young adults. But his muse was deserting him. A year's research on anti-Masonry failed to fructify; a planned Civil War novel petered out after just one installment in *The Saturday Evening Post*. The well was dry. His friend Bernard DeVoto later told him that early success is the worst thing that can happen to a writer—Edmonds agrees.

Edmonds came back nicely with the National Book Award–winning *Bert Breen's Barn* (1975), a novel for young adults. He is now at work, "haphazardly," on a series of vignettes about his early life with father.*

Mr. Edmonds is a solitary man, not given to schmoozing with the literati or chumming it up at writers conferences. Although he spearheaded the second great efflorescence of Yorker prose, he barely knew his comrades-in-arms Carl Carmer and Samuel Hopkins Adams, and knew Henry W. Clune not at all. There was, he says (and Mr. Clune concurs), no Upstate literary mafia as existed among, say, the Southern Agrarians. Certainly clannishness has its drawbacks, but we could have used our own *I'll Take My Stand* in the 1930s.

Mr. Edmonds tells a funny story about the first time he met Mr. Adams: "Samuel Hopkins Adams came up a couple of times to Northlands, our place [in Boonville]. He went all around the house on his first visit, saying what furniture was worth having and what was bogus. . . . He was a very

---

*Published as *Tales My Father Never Told* (Syracuse University Press, 1998).

forceful old boy. Most of the furniture there had been in my grandfather's house in Utica, so unless they were making spurious Victorian furniture in Utica. . . . [He was] without any animosity or scorn, he was just interested in it. My wife was trying to suppress a giggle and I felt much the same way."

Walter Edmonds was born five years too late to serve in the First World War; his work bears no trace of Lost Generation cynicism or world-weariness. Nor was he affected by the debunking stepchildren of the local colorists: he never even read Sherwood Anderson's *Winesburg, Ohio* or Edgar Lee Masters's *Spoon River Anthology*, and not until our Main Streets had been knocked down or boarded up did he acquaint himself with Sinclair Lewis.

"I'm not an intellectual," Mr. Edmonds insists. "I've always tried to make my characters real through their behavior, which I think is as good a way to judge a person as any. I don't try to practice psychiatry in their minds."

Among contemporary writers, he admires Eudora Welty above all. (In *One Writer's Beginnings*, Miss Welty writes that her father offered her mother a choice between living in Jackson, Mississippi, or the Thousand Islands. Of what literary riches were we deprived when Mrs. Welty made the wrong choice?)

Edmonds claims not to have had an overarching plan, but his oeuvre suggests otherwise. *Drums Along the Mohawk* shows us the settlement of the Mohawk Valley and the price of Independence; *Rome Haul* and *Erie Water* (1933) describe the canal, the first great stimulus to development; *Young Ames* (1942) and *Chad Hanna* (1940) give us Jacksonian America in all its enterprising, democratic exuberance; *The Big Barn* (1930) depicts agrarian New York at its pinnacle; and *The Boyds of Black River* (1953) traces the decline of the rural gentry. Edmonds had little interest in what came after: upon reaching the twentieth century, he turned his cart around and went back to the beginning, writing *The Musket and the Cross* (1968), a voluminous history of the struggle between the French and English for colonial America. Appropriately, Tom Dolan, the boy hero of *Bert Breen's Barn*, one of Edmonds's only excursions into our century, spends his time spelunking about an old barn, looking for a hidden nineteenth-century fortune.

The hallmarks of Edmonds's novels are a robust frontier humor and a respect for the pioneering virtues. His characters are plain people—Dan Harrows, Gil Martins—who by dint of hard work and native sense create a life and community in a big country.

A note of elegy plays through Edmonds's works. The agrarian, Jeffersonian New York that Edmonds sees as the Revolution's happy result is altered, in ways subtle and obvious, by the first great internal improvement of young America, the Erie Canal. When *Chad Hanna*'s Mrs. Huguenine says, referring to the Spirit of '76, "I wish I'd been born in that time. I'd have liked it," we are sure that she speaks for the author.

In *Rome Haul*, the appositely named Dan Harrow leaves his Tug Hill farm to make his fortune on the canal. He finds adventure, and a facsimile of love, but after a season or two he returns to the plow. At the outset of his journey, Harrow is befriended by a grizzled peddler, who hails the canal as "the bowels of the nation! It's the whole shebang of life!" The whore with whom he takes up warns Dan that "people live by different notions" on the canal, but Harrow plows ahead, mindful of the peddler's maxim that "canawlers keep a-moving." Tired of moving, deserted by his Molly, Dan leaves the canal to take a job superintending a dairy farm north of Boonville—where we find him ten years later in *The Big Barn*.

Dan Harrow is torn between the canal and the farm: he wants to be a yeoman, yet he also yearns for the footloose, independent life of a canaller. The vast farm that Harrow oversees in *The Big Barn* seems, as rootedness sometimes does, like a prison. How much more exciting—and, Edmonds suggests, ultimately meaningless—is the brawling, boozing, wenching life on the canal.

The Big Barn is an elemental tale of strong-willed tyrant Ralph Wilder, autocrat of 100,000 acres of the Black River Country. Ralph determines to build an immense barn that will be "bigger than the Ark," marvels one loafer at the general store. Ralph is pure action: "He'd own slaves down south, but he almost manages that up here anyway," observes his son Henry, a frail aesthete who has returned from Massachusetts with his wife, Rose Lane. (I had assumed "Rose Lane Wilder" was a nominative nod to the woman who persuaded her mother to write the *Little House on the Prairie* books; not so. "I've never read them," says Edmonds.)

Ralph Wilder's obsession with the barn is concomitant with a growing awareness of his mortality: "That barn will stand a while. . . . Maybe people will say who built it. That's something." Personal tragedies rob Ralph of his reason to believe: Henry is reported missing in the War Between the States, and his other son, Bascom, is killed by a cuckolded husband. The burden of the farm falls on Rose's shoulders; her life, suddenly, is informed by purpose. "The rhythm of daily labor had made its claim; she began to feel that she had always lived this daily round, that she would always live it. When Ralph was gone, she could see herself following it to the end, and her body growing older in the shadow of the barn." Rose may be Edmonds's fullest female character; Ralph is his most tragic.

For a man somewhat patronizingly known as a "canal writer," Edmonds can seem surprisingly ambivalent about Clinton's ditch. His third novel, *Erie Water*, is full of those minor characters that he drew so well—itinerants, preachers, snake-oil salesmen. They prophesy in dire tones about how the canal will destroy the old, and presumably honorable, way of life, and usher in a new world of bills and credit and debt and impersonality.

Erie Water follows a stout lad from Uniontown, Jerry Fowler, up and down the towpath. Fowler is enterprising and hard-working; in Edmonds's world, such qualities guarantee success. ("I'm a Horatio Alger type," admits Edmonds.) Jerry Fowler signs on to build locks, and labors so single-mindedly that his wife lights out, moving in with a farm family, the Hallecks, who remind one of prosperous Joads.

Erie Water is Edmonds's weakest novel; Jerry and his wife Mary are curiously lifeless, more ciceroni than characters. But the book nicely illustrates Edmonds's ambivalence about the canal, whose ardent fan he is said to be. Edmonds is nigh-reverent toward the sweat and toil off Irish and African brows that built the canal, and the seat-of-the-pants engineering and solid craftsmanship that undergird it. Nevertheless, the canal "is changing this whole land," the eldritch Merwin Gandy tells Jerry.

Gandy is a stock figure in the Edmonds repertory: one of those eccentrics, often a backwoodsman or itinerant preacher, who is part sage, part holy fool. *Erie Water* features a passel of rascals and their view of the creeping ditch is far from roseate. A salty farmer early on bemoans, "This canal ain't going to do me no good. . . . It's too far off. All they're going to do is tax me for it. Don't I pay high enough anyway? Here's my wife needing a new wheel and we're trying to get round to hire a schoolmaster now." Crack carpenter Self Rogers observes, "Afore this damned canal a man just said he'd work. Now he signs a paper. A man is captured and held legal." Snake-oil salesman cum Shaker Isachaar Bennet complains to Jerry of the declining sense of community now that progress has come: "It seems these people want to get to being gentrified. Learning is a splendid thing if you can take it just for knowledge. But to them it means money, setting up above your neighbors. One year a man will go to help his neighbor, Joe, nine miles off. Next year that same man's in a town, incorporated under statute, and he says, 'That Joe must be a backward man. He's still living under logs.' "

Finally even Jerry, monomaniacal canal builder Jerry, the classic ambitious poor boy on the make, has his doubts. Aboard a canal boat, pompous ass Vanderbilt Blue is bloviating about the progressive "vision" the canal represents. "I should think the diggers had the hardest job," Jerry offers. Blue scoffs, and points at a barn in the distance. "You don't want to look at that farm, nice as it is," he lectures. "That's not the wonder. The wonder is the canal that made this farm prosper." Edmonds concludes the scene: "But Jerry saw the barn."

The canal may be in some respects a baneful thing, an engine of unwanted progress, but it's also a monument to the toilers, to the workaday "Paddy on the Canal." Edmonds writes:

> Roberts wanted to see [the water pour into the canal] because of the shape it would have, the form for the picture he had seen in his mind's eye; the rodsmen and the axemen because it meant the end of their stay in this piece of wilderness; the cooks because it meant that they would no longer have to wash the plates of Irishmen and negroes. To the contractors it would mean profit or loss. To the farmers in Ohio it would mean a decent price for wheat. To the merchants in the east it would mean cheap transportation. Even in New York City it would mean money in the hope chest of Tammany Hall.
>
> His face lengthened.
>
> But to himself and to these wild Irishers, who had chopped at stumps, who had shoveled where half of each shovelful ran back at their toes, who had wheeled barrows, who had had the sun on their backs, the frost in their feet, the cold wet against their bellies, the ague and fever in their lungs, who had had stumps to pull, and piles to drive in quicksand, limestone to blast, and rock to devil which no force but their own could loosen, this water meant the sweat they had dropped in labor; it meant the blood of life in their veins; it meant the end of the job.

This marvelous feat of engineering and bullwork was the *ne plus ultra* of American Whiggery—never mind that the American System was a mere glint in Henry Clay's eye when the first shovel broke ground. The canal was what the Jeffersonians liked to call an "infernal improvement," a subsidy to the merchants who were gradually supplanting independent farmers as the backbone of the republic. The farm that transfixed Jerry Fowler is gone now. So is the prosperity that the canal brought. The bleakest vaticinations of Self Rogers and Merwin Gandy may not have been realized, but their decentralized agrarian republic lies a'moldering. (Actually, these cussed old men foresaw an Upstate very much like that depicted in Kurt Vonnegut's 1952 dystopian *Player Piano*. Set in Walter Edmonds territory, *Player Piano* presents an America in which craftsmanship and independence have vanished. The young men of Upper York—those not lucky enough to become mandarins in huge government-run corporations—are forced into the army or onto public-works crews performing make-work. The Jerry Fowlers of Vonnegut's Central New York are sots or insurrectionists; the Erie Water is spookily stagnant.)

In *The Boyds of Black River*, Edmonds's only post–Civil War novel for adults, a family dynasty is breathing its last. As the twentieth century impends, the Boyds, a once-great horse-racing family, are short of cash and thoroughbreds, reduced to "shabby gentility." They are revived by the arrival of the hoydenish Kathy O'Chelrie, a New York City actress who marries the final Boyd and brings life back to the old house and its inhabitants.

The Boyds of Black River tiptoes to the fin de siècle—there is talk of McKinley and that mad agrarian Bryan, and a newfangled motorcar is sighted, only to be outpaced by a horse—but Edmonds leaves us at the century's doorstep. The Boyds are set aright, treasury and stable enriched, but the author will take us no further. The twentieth century, with all its gadgetry and ideology, holds no allure for Walter Edmonds. He is rather like the Boyds' Uncle Ledyard, whose first encounter with the automobile is somewhat chary: "Uncle Ledyard got in and closed the door and said, 'Good morning,' to the chauffeur like a man saying good morning to Charon."

Still, life in the Black River country retains its charms. In one of the few instances in Edmonds's fiction in which the two New Yorks meet, New York City stage star Candida Brown visits the Boyd estate. She gushes: "You who've lived here all your lives have no idea how exciting it all is. It has a tang. It makes me think—do you know?—exactly of the first time I tasted caviar."

"You won't find any caviar in this house, my girl," [Admiral Porter] tells her dryly. "But Ledyard's got some whiskey that is damned good."

Edmonds's most exuberant character is the eponymous Chad Hanna, a "do-nothing, no-account" who is closer to a Yorker Huck Finn than a diligent Dan Harrow. Loafing around Canastota, Chad stumbles on the Underground Railroad, saves a slave, and joins a two-bit circus as it traverses the state from Albany to Albion.

The year is 1836: Jackson is preparing to pass the wand to Van Buren, a depression is around the corner, and sectional rancor is swelling. Chad, we feel certain, will choose the Union a quarter century later, with the same reluctance with which he saves the runaway. "I'm not no abolitionist," he avers—no pinch-cheeked Mrs. Grundy reproving drunks and caning hellions—but "the business [of emancipation] might have some fun in it." With the same lack of high-mindedness, rural New Yorkers marched off to war not long after.

Chad Hanna showcases Edmonds the storyteller. We get somersaults, horse stealing, a dog-toothed boy, and a lion revived with mineral water. Chad is a rounded, full-bodied character, unlike, say, Jerry Fowler of *Erie Water.*

The supporting cast in *Chad Hanna* is boisterous fun. An Edmonds stock character, the wizened wry oldster, is here in the form of Revolutionary pensioner/idler Elias Proops, who tells lovelorn Chad, "The way I've always looked at marriage, it's all right except you've got to live with a woman." Of an inept Italian juggler and his new assistant, someone says, "She makes a good partner for Fiero. I always said there wasn't no sense to a man tossing balls all alone. He's crazy about her. He wants to throw knives at her too, now."

And yet the old Edmonds ambivalence about progress pops up here and there. Circus agent Mr. Bisbee muses, "I remember how we used to cuss the mud and wish for solid roads. Well, we're getting the roads, and look what they're doing to us. They've turned us into a little show, and a thing has to be expensive now before it can be a genuine wonder."

Mrs. Huguenine, the wife of the circus's impresario, tells the roustabout after he's fallen in love with the daughter of a slave-catcher: "A man oughtn't really to get married unless he's saved up fifty dollars. In the old times, you didn't need cash money. You got a cow off your parents and you took up free land with an axe and a rifle. . . . But nowadays it's difficult. Folks are trading in stores for their food and they spend money on their clothes."

Only once—apart from his novels for young adults, notably *Cadmus Henry* (1949), the tale of a green Confederate balloonist—has Edmonds ventured outside his native ground: the result was *Young Ames*, a critically panned work that Edmonds says he wrote "just to make money when the college bills were due."

John Ames is an ambitious, orphaned boy from Troy bent on making his fortune in New York City. He is taken on as an errand-runner at a trading house; through pluck, adolescent sagacity, and a dash of unscrupulous rascality he succeeds in business and love. This is Horatio Alger, with a Yorker twist, and if one accepts the implausibilities it is an amusing read.

"It was great fun writing it," recalls Edmonds. "I know nothing about business; I have no sense of finance. I had a book called *Merchants of Old*

New York and I got a lot of stuff out of that. It was perfectly ridiculous, but everyone took it seriously."

Young Ames is not one of Edmonds's stronger efforts, but it hardly deserves execration. The figure of Andrew Jackson is always hovering in the background. Young Ames's boss, the Federalist Mr. Chevalier, despises Jackson; Ames himself exemplifies the energetic spirit of Jacksonian America. (Indeed, the boy impersonated Old Hickory's nephew at one point on a Southern sojourn.) Historians have long recognized the protean face of Jacksonianism: its style was frontier, egalitarian, demotic, but through their laissez-faire economic policies the Jacksonians liberated a new entrepreneurial class. They were capitalists of a sort; bitterly opposed to Nicholas Biddle's National Bank but eager to make the economic clime conducive to success for ambitious young men of few means like Young John Ames.

In a scene that Edmonds carries off with admirable facility, John meets Old Hickory on a trip to Washington. The boy is undaunted and bold, much to the president's pleasure. Jackson expounds upon American principles and even tosses in some lagniappe advice on how to propose to a girl. Ames's "ambition," writes Edmonds, "was the same instinct . . . that raised a man like Andrew Jackson out of obscure beginnings."

Edmonds himself is a Jefferson–Jackson man whose name shall ever be tied to the Whiggish canal. But for the most part, his characters are resolutely apolitical. (Or antipolitical.) When a taproom Whig firebrand demands of Chad Hanna, "How do you stand on Masonry?" he replies coolly, "I don't stand on anything but my own feet."

The utopian and reform fires that burned over our district in the first half of the nineteenth century do not so much as singe the Edmonds corpus. Joseph Smith makes a cameo appearance in *Erie Water*: he is said to have "shifty eyes" and he makes Jerry Fowler "queasy." Jemima Wilkinson, John Humphrey Noyes, the ladies of Seneca Falls: they are absent from Walter Edmonds's Upstate of plain people. Chad Hanna enlists, on a whim, in the cause of abolition, but only because the slave-freeing business "might have some fun in it." A pity that Edmonds never got a handle on his anti-Masonry novel: What would his earthy pragmatists have made of the millenarian fanatics and shrewd operators who rode the Blessed Spirit to Congress and the state legislature in the 1830s?

The Civil War looms throughout in the background of *The Big Barn* (and *Cadmus Henry*, which takes place in Virginia). Ralph Wilder and the boys are gung-ho war hawks, as is Edmonds, for a familial reason: "One of my ancestors, Samuel Joseph May, a Unitarian minister in Syracuse, was a leading abolitionist and a great friend of Gerritt Smith and Frederick Douglass. He kept what I am told was the fastest buggy in Syracuse, and all the time he didn't allow his wife more than a candle to sew by. She went blind, but he kept his horseflesh up to standards because he ran the main underground station in Syracuse. At night he would take one or two slaves in his buggy and run north."

There was significant Copperhead sentiment in these parts, so it's apt that Edmonds's predecessor, Harold Frederic, depicted antiwar Democratic farmers sympathetically in works such as *The Copperhead.* Frederic was an admirer of his fellow Utican, Governor Horatio Seymour, a principled opponent of the federal government's suspension of habeas corpus and other circumventions of the Constitution.

Edmonds disclaims any didactic intent in his novels, although in the introduction to *Drums Along the Mohawk* he wrote: "To those who may feel that here is a great to-do about a bygone life, I have one last word to say. It does not seem to me a bygone life at all. The parallel is too close to our own. The people of the valley were confronted by a reckless Congress and ebullient finance, with their inevitable repercussions of poverty and practical starvation. They suffered the paralysis of abject dependence on a central government totally unfitted to comprehend a local problem. And finally, though they had lost two thirds of their fighting strength, these people took hold of their courage and struck out for themselves."

He wrote that, he says, as an Upstate Republican worried over the centralizing trends of the New Deal. He was never much on politicos, although Thomas E. Dewey once asked him to write his campaign biography. "I was rather incensed," remembers Edmonds. "I'd sort of believed in Dewey [and his] statements to the press that he wouldn't betray the people of New York by running for president." It is a measure of Walter Edmonds's gentlemanliness that he was genuinely surprised when a politician reneged on a promise.

Walter Edmond's accomplishment is enormous and underknown. He has fictionalized the history of Upstate New York from the Revolution till the dawn of our industrial century. An Edmonds anthology referred to his books as "stalwarts," reliable draft horses, but his prose was touched with felicity too. No naive singer of bucolic charms, he nevertheless gloried in "the shape of the land with its even trim, the little curves and hollows that the eye would never trace in grass; and in itself it showed the sweeps of the sower's hand, sweeps like the curve of the scythe blade where the seed had fallen, taken root, made milk and grain, been reaped—a cycle for the eye to grasp in a single glimpse."

His pioneers are practical, earthy men and women. They are giants in the earth, embodying what Lionel D. Wyld, in *Walter D. Edmonds, Storyteller* (1982), called the "Yorker-based philosophy of individual worth and dignity, of commonsense approaches to the problems of living, and of simple pleasures which sometimes show how very close sadness is to laughter, tragedy to comedy."

Edmonds's generation—his coevals include Edmund Wilson, Rochester novelist Henry W. Clune, and *Saturday Evening Post* short-story writer George Brooks of Pearl Creek—had a self-confidence, a sureness that their home was a region of worth and dignity, a self-governing bulwark of the American republic. Edmonds, Clune, and Wilson were no strangers to elegy: none was overly taken with the modernized Upstate struggling to be born. Their dirges sound ever more plaintive today. When Henry Clune wondered in 1930 whether "the old spirit of neighborliness that gave such a distinct character to the average residential street before the advent of the motor car, the movie and other institutions of the present era that tend to take people out of and away from their homes, anywhere exists," he was rephrasing the fears of Self Rogers and other cussed independents in the Edmonds ensemble.

When Edmund Wilson, the cranky sage of Talcottville who envied Edmonds the acceptance of the locals, mourned, "I have come to feel that this country, whether or not I live in it, is no longer any place for me," he could've been Isaachar Bennet watching the canal cut its swath through the virgin forest.

(Wilson told Edmonds to his face that he found his books "terribly dull" but thought him unequaled in writing about animals. He fiddled with a piece for *The New Yorker* along these lines, but nothing, apparently, ever came of it. Alas.)

"It's been going downhill so fast," says Mr. Edmonds of his country. "I am appalled at the widening between poverty and extreme wealth [and] the corrupting of the American Dream, which never was getting a lot of money. It was getting independence, the ability to lead your life as you wanted to lead it, do your business the way you wanted to do it. But it didn't mean getting money, money, money all the time." (Edmonds's distaste for the latter part of our bloody century has concrete roots. His childhood home in New York City—"the old Federal house on 11th Street"—was blown up on March 6, 1970, by the infamous Weatherman homemade pipe-bomb explosion.)

What a contrast Edmonds, Clune, and company make with the youngest generation of New York writers—we who were bequeathed a Thruwayed, Rockefellered, Atticaed, television-blinded Upstate. Mistah Hanna, he dead. You can find him in an unmarked mass grave, buried with Natty Bumppo and David Harum and Theron Ware.

We drove back along Governor Dewey's Erie Canal, the New York State Thruway, which has inspired no fiction, no romance, no Walter Edmonds. As the canal destroyed the Upstate of Self Rogers, the Thruway killed the York of small shopkeepers and self-contained towns along that old Indian trail, Routes 5 and 20. I rolled down the window and listened for a lonesome drum, but all I heard was the whoosh of rushing cars, and all I saw was a sky of gray.

But gloom passes. I recalled the opening scene of *Rome Haul*: Dan Harrow and the old peddler arrive in Boonville and behold the welcoming brick of the Hurlburt House. Decades later, Frederick Exley, in his toper chronicle *Pages from a Cold Island* (1975), fantasizes about owning none other than that selfsame Hurlburt House. Perhaps the novels of Walter Edmonds offer us a roadmap. In the words of T. S. Eliot: "And the end of all our exploring / Will be to arrive where we started / And know the place for the first time."

3

Barber B. Conable Jr.

Our Statesman, 2021

Barber Conable at his Wooton desk. Courtesy of Common Cause.

In 2018, Jane Schmieder, one of the four children of Charlotte and Barber Conable, asked if I'd like to be the first person to read her late father's congressional diaries in their entirety. A friend and longtime admirer of Mr. Conable's—though, as I explain in chapter 17 of this book, on the election of 1974, I got my start in politics by sticking flyers under windshield wipers for his strongest opponent, Midge Costanza—I jumped at the chance. I wound up editing the diaries, which the University Press of Kansas published in 2021 as The Congressional Journal of Barber B. Conable, Jr., 1968–1984. The essay below is drawn from my Introduction to that book.

Barber Benjamin Conable Jr. was "as highly and widely respected as any member of Congress in the last half of the twentieth century," according to Richard Fenno, the late dean of congressional scholars and author of the classic *Home Style: House Members in Their Districts* (1978).

Conable was a rectitudinous rural intellectual of the sort once produced by the muck-spattered gentry. He grew up reciting Browning and Gray with his father as they milked the cows. He was a small-town lawyer, a youthful pacifist who enlisted in the Marines and fought at Iwo Jima, yet he never exploited his heroism for political gain. Though he served twenty years (1965–1985) in the US House of Representatives, Conable was so deeply rooted in his district that he became the avatar of rural Western New York.

A Republican pragmatist with a localist streak, Conable was a self-described "Jeffersonian decentralist," who nevertheless believed strongly in the two-party system. He was ranking Republican on the Ways and Means Committee during the Carter and the first Reagan administrations, his party's spokesman on tax policy, and a father of Nixon-era revenue sharing. Although he would solidify a reputation as a moderate Republican, mostly for his support of the Equal Rights Amendment and various civil-rights measures, Conable was parsimonious on budgetary matters and a relatively strict constructionist with respect to the Constitution. Unshakably honest, Conable refused campaign contributions of greater than $50, joking that he could be "bought more cheaply" than anyone in Congress.

For seventeen of his years in the House, Barber Conable kept a journal in which he recorded his thoughts, his actions, his opinions, and his doubts. He spoke this into a Dictaphone while driving himself to and from work on Capitol Hill, and also on the long drive between Washington and his home in Alexander, New York. Comprising upward of 400,000 words, Conable's journal is literate, searching, ruminative, brutally frank, self-lacerating, sometimes amusing and elsetimes dripping with asperity.

There are no advertisements for himself therein, nor is there a hint of self-aggrandizement. The journal is a unique entry on the sparsely populated shelf of congressional diaries, containing the impressions of a very bright, hardworking, conscientious representative surrounded by some men and women of talent and quality, some dullards, some blowhards, and on every side overweening ambition.

This is how Congress works, or how it worked from the late 1960s through the mid-1980s. We read of the hashing out of differences, the personalizing of conflicts, the workhorses and the show horses. We learn, from an angle of vision not found in any civics text (is there such a thing anymore as a civics text?) how a bill becomes (or doesn't become) a law.

The journal includes keenly drawn portraits of the lions of both House and Senate of his era: such figures as Daniel Patrick Moynihan (with whom Conable had a relationship of mutual admiration and occasional exasperation); John Anderson (who exhausted Conable's initial admiration); Jack Kemp (whom Conable never admired; you can almost see him roll his eyes and sigh ruefully whenever the frenetic Kemp makes an appearance); longtime Ways and Means Committee chairman Wilbur Mills, the shrewd Arkansan whose slow-motion dissolution (ending in embarrassing scandal) we witness through Conable's eyes; and a cast of hundreds. He is thoroughly bipartisan in his evaluations. There are Republicans (Bill Frenzel of Minnesota, Bill Steiger of Wisconsin) and Democrats (Abner Mikva of Illinois, Jim Corman of California, Richard Bolling of Missouri) whom he esteems throughout, and there are others—Sam Gibbons (D-FL) is a particularly interesting case—whom Conable only comes to value after extended exposure thereto.

He draws incisive portraits and issues candid assessments of the Republican presidents with whom he worked. Conable had endorsed his home-state Governor Nelson Rockefeller in the Republican presidential nomination contest of 1968, considering Richard Nixon "a plate of warmed-over hash," yet he became a key Nixon ally, rather to his later mortification. His support of Nixon, he told me, was due to the president's "decentralist" bent, as evidenced by his promotion of revenue sharing, but Conable's Watergate-driven disillusionment was severe and irrevocable. He refused to answer the postpresidential Nixon's missives and spoke harshly of his dishonesty.

We follow Gerald Ford in these pages from his position as House minority leader into the vice presidency (Betty Ford blamed Conable for her husband's ascension) and then the presidency. Conable supported Ford for the 1976 GOP nomination over Ronald Reagan, and he would consistently underestimate Reagan's political appeal and prospects, the wish perhaps being father to the thought. He was chairman of the national steering committee of his former Ways and Means colleague George H. W. Bush's 1980 presidential campaign, and Conable's excitement at Bush's selection as Reagan's running mate is palpable. Bush's failure as vice president to assume a more forceful role as a voice of moderation disappointed Conable, and the two would suffer a break in relations in later years when Bush was president of the United States and Conable was president of the World Bank, a post to which Ronald Reagan appointed him in 1986. Conable would say of Bush, "He thought I should be supporting an American agenda; I thought I was there to help the poor people. So I got the reputation of not being a team player, and that was the one thing George wouldn't stand for."

Barber Benjamin Conable Jr. was born November 2, 1922, in Warsaw, New York, a village of 4,400, the seat of a county (Wyoming) in which cows have long outnumbered people. An ancestor, Samuel Conable Jr., had settled in Warsaw in 1817, eventually building up a woolen manufactory. Samuel's mother, Sarah, was the daughter of Thomas Crafts, one of the "True Born Sons of Liberty" and both a participant in and supplier of the Mohawk dress for the Boston Tea Partiers. Samuel Sr. and Sarah bore the surname Cunnabell, which the subsequent generation shortened.

Samuel Jr.'s brother, Rufus Conable, and Rufus's wife, Sophia, made the trek from New England to Western New York in 1821. Rufus was a farmer and tavern keep; his son Benjamin Barber Conable farmed and was a partner in a lumber and building materials company with, among others, Augustus Frank, Civil War–era Republican congressman from Warsaw and an influential promoter of the Thirteenth Amendment.

In the next generation of what had become by then one of the leading families of Wyoming County, Barber Benjamin Conable Sr. would graduate Cornell in 1901, receive his law degree from New York University, and practice in the village of Warsaw. He married Agnes Gouinlock, who bore three sons, the youngest being Barber Benjamin Conable Jr.

In 1923, Barber Sr. was elected Wyoming County Judge. He would serve in that position for twenty-eight years, the longest tenure in the history of the county—until it was surpassed by his son John, Barber Jr.'s brother, who was elected to succeed his father in 1951 and did not leave office until thirty-two years later. (Barber's eldest brother, William Gouinlock Conable, was an attorney and Buffalo-area civil rights activist who died in 1966.)

The Conable family lived, appositely, on Jefferson Street.

Young Barber hated his forename. He was teased by classmates with an old nursery rhyme.

> Barber, barber, shave a pig!
> How many hairs will make a wig?
> Four and twenty; that's enough
> Give the Barber a pinch of snuff.

Still, its distinctiveness would come in handy for the candidate. During Barber's first congressional race, a barbershop quartet of young women sang for him, and even late into his career some of his less attentive constituents were sure that they were represented by a nice lady named Barbara.

Barber's native Warsaw had been singed by the fires of what became known to historians as the "Burned-Over District" of Upstate New York, hotbed of numerous reform movements of antebellum America. The Conable family was touched by those flames. In 1839, Warsaw hosted a convention of the New York Anti-Slavery Society that laid the groundwork for the formation of the abolitionist Liberty Party; Warsaw-based congressmen Seth Gates and Augustus Frank were among the most ardent of congressional abolitionists. Coincidentally—or aptly—Jane Conable Schmieder, Barber's daughter, practiced law with partner Charlotte Smallwood-Cook—who had married Barber's cousin Ned Smallwood; the small-town web is tangled—in the two-story Italian villa-style residence that had been the home of Congressman Frank.

Barber's mother and his grandmother, Margaret Gouinlock, were suffragists; his grandmother was a close friend of Susan B. Anthony's. "So I came by [my feminism] honestly," he said. "I wasn't just being a milquetoast for my wife's enthusiasm."

Barber Conable Sr. drilled his boys in the fundamentals of civic and personal responsibility, though his lessons were leavened with a dollop of agrarian eccentricity. Barber Jr. recalled that his father recited Walter Scott's *The Lady of the Lake* and other verse from memory while milking: "My father thought it was good for a young man's character to have to clean out the stables. Our cows used to give better to iambic pentameter. They were the most productive cows in Wyoming County."

Barber Jr. attended Cornell, where he majored in medieval history and helped to organize the antiwar America First Committee. Like his father, he was a pacifist who opposed US involvement in foreign wars. Among his notable America First classmates at Cornell was the future novelist Kurt Vonnegut, who in later years "used to lobby me about getting more deductions for authors." (Even socialists prefer their taxes as low as possible.)

Conable graduated Cornell in 1942 at the age of nineteen, enlisted (over the "bitter" objections of his pacifist father) in the Marines as a private, and went ashore as a second lieutenant at Iwo Jima on February 19, 1945, his father's birthday. He told his biographer Jim Fleming that he remembered thinking, as he landed on the beach at the base of Mount Suribachi, "My God, I'm going to be killed on my father's birthday." He received not even a scratch. After the war, Conable earned a law degree at Cornell, serving as editor of *The Cornell Law Review* and graduating first in his class.

Following an unhappy stint with a prestigious Buffalo law firm (he "hated" corporate tax law) and an eighteen-month detour as a stateside intelligence officer during the Korean War, Conable and his new bride, Charlotte Williams, a Buffalo native and Cornell graduate, moved to Batavia, twenty miles north of Warsaw. This seat of neighboring Genesee County was a burg of just under 18,000 souls. Brother John had been elected Wyoming County judge, and Barber "wasn't about to put myself in the position where all my life I'd have to practice in my brother's court."

The newcomer jumped into civic affairs as if he were auditioning for a role in a Sinclair Lewis novel. He was active in Boy Scouts, United Fund, Chamber of Commerce, and, critically, the Rotary Club.

In short order he was named to the Republican city committee, then "within three months I was selected chairman of the city committee because nobody wanted it."

After Barber and Charlotte bought a circa 1830 hybrid Federal–Greek Revival home in Alexander, the town south of Batavia, he agreed to serve as Genesee County campaign chairman in the 1960 election. Two years later he refused the county GOP chairman's request to reprise his role. "I won't be campaign chairman if that old bastard Austin Erwin is on the ticket," he told Party chairman Jim Beach, "because he's a crook." Beach warned Conable that he was throwing away his career if he challenged Erwin, the powerful chairman of the State Senate Finance Committee; Conable, with the support of the Batavia *Daily News* and "a bunch of young punks from the Republican committee," threw his hat in the ring.

In announcing his candidacy in April 1962 he explained: "I consider myself a conservative, and while I acknowledge that no governmental problem is simple, I can generally be expected to favor that course which encourages responsibility in our localities, rather than vesting additional power in our distant seats of government." He also pledged "not to use my public position for private gain."

Erwin backed down from the challenge; Conable was elected to the state senate, routing an Erwin protégé in the GOP primary. In his maiden race, Conable won 329 of the 346 votes cast in Alexander—a ringing endorsement by his neighbors.

Two years later, in the teeth of Barry Goldwater's landslide defeat, Conable was easily elected to the US House of Representatives, succeeding GOP backbencher Harold Ostertag.

Barber Conable distinguished himself almost immediately by reviving a practice that was seemingly as dead as the peruke and the snuff box: that of writing one's own newsletter to his or her constituents.

He explained: "In Kierkegaard's phrase, you try to get to a truth that's true for you. That's particularly true in politics. One way to have an unsuccessful political career is to imitate somebody. So I tried to develop my own formula, and it involved writing my own newsletter, which I did every three weeks and wrote every word of it myself."

Conable mailed these more-or-less monthly newsletters not to everyone in the district, as is typical, but rather to those "who were interested in Congress" and who requested to be placed on the list. At its peak these numbered about 30,000 recipients.

Senator Daniel Patrick Moynihan (D-NY) once said that he admired Conable above all members of Congress, not least for Conable's newsletters, which contained none of the usual self-promoting guff. They were pedagogical, introspective, even confessional. (Moynihan tried to emulate Conable in this respect, but he lacked the discipline.)

The new congressman also cut a distinctive profile in his fundraising beliefs and practices. As early as 1966 he was proposing to cap congressional campaign spending at ten cents per constituent, which would have meant about $45,000 per candidate. Appalled by the contributions-for-favors relationship between lobbyists and some members of the Ways and Means Committee, he set a strict limit of $50 on gifts to his own campaigns. Conable's interest in campaign-finance reform eventually led him to assume leadership of the small GOP faction that supported public financing of congressional candidates. His Republican critics noted that Conable hadn't need of a large war chest, as he had only one difficult race in his career: that of the Watergate year of 1974, when feisty Rochester vice mayor Margaret "Midge" Costanza made an energetic and well-financed run (she outspent Conable nearly two-to-one) against him.

Barber Conable joined the Ways and Means Committee in 1967, in just his second term, and was widely regarded as a promising young man. He was labeled a moderate, though that limp term doesn't really do justice to or accurately capture Conable's blend of fiscal parsimony, institutional reformism, Burned-Over District social liberalism, hard-headed realism, solicitude for Main Street, constitutional federalism, and strong preference for local and voluntaristic solutions rather than top-down programs. He insisted that "the Republican Party is a middle class and not a business party." Very quickly he became a leader of the free-trade bloc in a party that, in its pre-Reagan incarnation, retained a substantial and traditionally Republican protectionist wing.

He would serve his entire career as a member of the minority party in the House, a source of discouragement for him, especially under the Ways and Means chairmanship of Rep. Dan Rostenkowski (D-IL), whom Conable regarded as a petty man, a wily politician, and a bully.

In *Federalist* 52, James Madison wrote that a member of the US House of Representatives should have an "an intimate sympathy" with the people whom he represents. Conable, by dint of lineage, upbringing, and disposition, had an almost mystical connection to his district—in particular to its rural and small-town portion.

Political scientist Richard Fenno, who disguised Conable as "Congressman H" in *Home Style*, grasped his placedness, his ubiety, right from the start. They met in November 1964, when Fenno, a professor at the University of Rochester, was on assignment from *The New York Times Magazine* to profile newly elected representatives. (*The Times Magazine*, which Gore Vidal called the graveyard of American prose, killed the piece.) Conable explained his politics at their first meeting: "We're all decentralists up here. We don't trust the big cities and the impersonal government way off somewhere. We like our local institutions."

Traveling with Conable in spring 1970, as he was researching what became *Home Style*, Fenno discerned the congressman's essence: "From the time we spent driving through the district during that first visit, I picked up something more basic and more permanent—his attachment to a place—and to the values and practices of that place." As Conable drove Fenno from Rochester, whose western edge made up about one-third of the district, into the countryside, he spoke of what home meant to him. Fenno wrote:

> [H]is comment to me about his identification with the rural people of his district was almost poetic in nature, because it came just as we left the four-lane superhighway . . . and turned onto the two-lane road to (small town) Byron . . . Suddenly, he said, "It must be terrible to be without roots, without a place to call home. I have a profound sense of identification with these rural people: . . . I worry about the rootlessness of our people, about the changes that are taking place in our values which were, after all, pretty durable." Soon, he brightened and said, "It won't be long now. Here are the Byron suburbs! Those are Gerald Britt's beets growing over there. He grows 3 percent of all the edible beets in the United States."

Conable had an aw-shucks side, but it was authentic, not a politician's calculating put-on. Fenno writes: "[D]uring my first visit Conable displayed another personal behavior pattern that distinguished him from every elective politician I would ever know. It was a distinctiveness related partly to shared rural, small-town values/expectations and partly to his self-confidence in connecting with his constituents. Not once in all our time together did a staff person accompany us—not in the car and not at any event."

Though popular, Conable was never completely comfortable in those sections of his district comprising the city of Rochester and its suburbs. He explained, "In the urban area, I'm a captive of the party. I go to rallies and stand up and make platitudinous pro-party solidarity statements. I'm not allowed to be independent, to be myself. People in the rural areas wouldn't be satisfied with this. They expect whole relationships with people, not fragmentary relationships the way city people do. I like whole relationships, and that's why I do so much better in the rural area than in the urban area."

"I'm a country boy and Rochester is a sophisticated enclave," he once said to me, wink in eye and tongue in cheek, as this habitue of the opera and the theater, this reciter of poetry—and not doggerel—from memory, this avid listener to "Schubert, Mozart, Haydn, Verdi, and Beethoven," was no slack-jawed yokel.

As the years went by, the plaudits for Barber Conable piled up. A *National Journal* profile remarked: "House members, lobbyists and journalists speak admiringly of him, more because of his intellectual brilliance than because of his expertise." Bob Woodward and Carl Bernstein, in *The Final Days*, said that "he was regarded by his colleagues as almost puritanical in his standards of personal and political conduct, a man of unquestioned integrity." George Will concluded that "There has never been a better congressman."

Conable declined to seek reelection in 1984, but he never gave a thought to stepping into the meretricious role of lobbyist. He said to me, "Now why would I stick around Washington? That's what many of my colleagues do: they stay there and practice law or lobby. . . . And that's one of the most foolish things in the world. There's nothing deader than a dead politician. I recall my dear friends Wilbur Mills and Al Ullman coming to lobby me after they had gone to their rewards one way or another, and I would duck into doorways to avoid them because they would be asking me for things that I knew they didn't believe in. They were pure mercenaries."

The "toughest job" he turned down, he said, "was an endowed chair at Harvard, in the Kennedy School of Government. I seriously considered that for a long time, and finally I said to my wife, 'You know, here I am, sixty-one years old. I was asked to buy a very expensive house in a Boston suburb, get a great big mortgage, buck a whole new traffic pattern, establish a whole new set of friends, start on a whole new career I don't know whether I'd be any good at.' " When, a year and a half later, he was offered the presidency of the World Bank, he thought that "the opportunity to be useful on a global level" was "a very tempting one. So I did accept that."

Upon leaving the World Bank in 1991 after a single five-year term, Barber Conable returned home to Alexander, though he remained active as chairman of the executive committee of the Board of Regents of the Smithsonian Institution and as chairman of the National Committee on US-China Relations. For the next dozen years he would move seamlessly between worlds: one night he might be chairing the Smithsonian Regents, and the next night he and Charlotte were discussing with fellow members of the Holland Purchase Historical Society—"the Hysterical Society," they jokingly called it—how much to spend on toner cartridges. Mr. Conable manned the cashbox at the society's annual yard sale. As museum director Pat Weissend joked to him, Conable was qualified for this job by virtue of having been "a teller at the World Bank."

He gave, by his count, ten to fifteen talks a year on local history and culture. They were witty, informative, extemporaneous, and of course gratis. By long tradition he continued to read the Declaration of Independence every Fourth of July at the Genesee Country Village and Museum (Upstate's Williamsburg), and he kept his date most Saturday mornings, as he had since 1952, for "coffee with the boys" at Genesee Hardware, whose proprietor Karl Buchholtz had long ago propelled him into Batavia's Rotary Club. He also planted 187 varieties of trees on the three acres behind his home in Alexander. ("I'm a tree hugger," he confessed.)

The last time I saw Barber Conable he spoke, plaintively, about the ephemeral nature of his legislative accomplishments, likening them to footprints on a sandy beach, washed away by the tide, with nary a sign that they'd ever been there. His most lasting achievement, he said with bemusement, seemed to be his authorship of the provision in the 1978 tax bill that effectively legalized home brewing and made him the legislative father of the microbrewery revolution. Conable never even mentions this in his journal, and when asked about it a quarter century later by two journalists, he said simply, "I did not consider it a big deal."

Barber Conable died on November 30, 2003. Charlotte passed in 2013. Their stone is in the Alexander Village Cemetery, on whose board of trustees Barber served. The Conable plot is in the western verge of the cemetery, adjacent to a pasture. "He wanted the Schmieder cows to come to his funeral," said his daughter Emily. The couple is commemorated with a black marble bench on which is incised the message "Reach Out!"

Every May the village of Alexander is brilliant with flowering crabapple trees that line its streets. These were a gift from Barber Conable. As his daughter Jane explained, "He loved Alexander. He was so enormously attached to that place as his home that he wanted to give it a beautiful gift and pay it back, at the same time making it more beautiful with its own special identity."

4

John Gardner

This Bud's for Us, 2003

John Gardner. Collection of Bill Kauffman.

I started my first novel at 19, in direct response to a Jewish girl from New York City who hated "apple-knockers." That's what she called upstate New Yorkers. She liked me but figured I was an exception. Of course, I wasn't. I had the same prejudices—Republican, Protestant, the whole thing. So I tried to present a rich vision of the apple-knocker world, openly and honestly. I felt when I finished it that the girl would have to think after reading the novel that apple-knockers were OK if you took time to understand them.

—John Gardner

The novelist John Champlin Gardner (1933–1982) was Batavia's only contribution to the national arts and letters. (I write while winking.) His works include ten novels, most notably *Grendel*, *The Sunlight Dialogues*, and *October Light*; several books of advice for aspiring writers; and *On Moral Fiction*, a notorious polemic against what he regarded as the enfeebled and amoral state of contemporary literature.

Gardner, one of the last major American writers to grow up on a farm (perhaps the last, given the disappearance of rural America), lived in a brick farmhouse on a rise in the Putnam Settlement Road just outside Batavia. The family homestead, as he wrote in his magnum opus *The Sunlight Dialogues*, was "solid, unspeakably dignified with its great blunt planes of chalky orange brick, its Victorian porches, its cupola: the most beautiful architecture in the world, symbolic of virtues no longer to be found." The hillock on which the house sits drops slantwise to the road and was "full of snakes," says a family friend with a shiver.

"Bud," as Gardner was known to family and friends, was an Eagle Scout who played in the band and sang in the chorus at Alexander Central School before graduating from Batavia High in 1951. He had transferred to BHS in order to study with music director Frank Owen, whose son, Jim, coached my MacArthur Park midget baseball team in 1969.

Ask a Gardner coeval about the author and you'll hear one word: *weird*. As a child he loved books and opera; as an adult, he was seen roaming the sepulchral Genesee Country Mall in a black cape, like Merlin in search of a vodka and tonic. Gardner meant a lot to me: He was my Joe Louis, my Al Smith, living proof that a lad from Batavia was not debarred from Parnassus, or a suburb thereof. But, I admit, he was weird.

As a weirdo he did not shun the beaux arts; I think of him lugging that French horn to Batavia High, to the sniggering of the jocks who forever taunt band geeks. I find in a 1950 Batavia *Daily News* clip that seventeen-year-old John Gardner Jr. sang with a "quartet composed of young people" to the First Presbyterian Friendly Class. He later lied (he told whoppers that put his close friend and compulsive fabulist James Dickey to shame) that he had been a motorcycle champion, a regular Burned-Over District Marlon Brando, but he was nothing of the sort. No, John was a winds weenie, his photo nowhere to be found on the football or baseball or basketball pages of the Alexander and Batavia High yearbooks. (He did go out for track, the sport of those culled from the baseball team. His specialty? The longueur jump.)

For all the cow shit and June bugs that flavor Gardner's autobiographical reminiscences, his family were among Batavia's oldest and most accomplished. Great-great-grandfather Moses Taggert was a justice of the New York Supreme Court. His granddaughter—John's grandmother, Alice Day Gardner—was the first woman to practice law in Batavia. Alice cofounded the Children's Home, whose ministry to orphans was subsidized for so many years by Madam Edna, Batavia's brothel keep, who appears briefly in *The Sunlight Dialogues.*

Alice's husband Fred—the model for the Honorable Arthur Hodge Sr. in *The Sunlight Dialogues*—was a reporter for the *Daily News* before joining the bar; his funeral, prominently covered in his old paper, was attended "in a body" by Batavia Lodge No. 475, Free and Accepted Masons. An earlier John Champlin Gardner, among the first settlers in Elba in 1809, served in the New York State Assembly.

The Gardner farm was not run on Earl Butz-Archer Daniels Midland hyperefficiency principles. Priscilla, John's mother, was an English teacher, and his father, John Sr., was a loquacious lay preacher: they recited *King Lear* and the Psalms to each other as they milked the cows. The Gardners were famous at the Grange for giving their farmhands Saturday afternoons off so that the boys might listen to the Texaco opera on the radio. Just how many did so was never clear. After all, you can lead a hoss to Wagner, but you can't . . .

When you grow up hearing dairy farmers whistling Walter Scott before dawn you understand that high culture might be shared by muck-spattered workaday men lacking graduate degrees. Thus Gardner's oft-derided habit of putting poetic language or classical allusions in mouths that never have supped in faculty clubs. The drunk junkman Kuzitski quotes Pope in Henry Soames's diner in *Nickel Mountain*; Gardner's farmers and farmwives are always reciting poetry and reading to each other (or to the kine). Ruth Thomas is "sitting on a milkstool" and reading Poe and Wilkie Collins in *October Light*, while old man Orrick (who "owned a small dairy farm a mile outside the little village of Elba") composes poetry on his tractor in the posthumously published *Stillness.*

Verse in the cowbarn is as natural to Gardner as was his use of pipe words like "dottle" or his casual mention of the inevitable farming accidents that cost Gardnerian characters their fingers, their hands, their lives.

"Art begins in a wound, an imperfection," wrote Gardner in *On Moral Fiction*, "and is an attempt either to learn to live with the wound or to heal it. It is the pain of the wound which impels the artist to do his work." Gardner suffered his wound on April 4, 1945, and we can be sure that it never healed.

Let the *Daily News* provide the facts.

CHILD DIES IN FALL FROM FARM TRACTOR

6½-Year-Old Son of Mr. and Mrs. John C. Gardner Is Killed Instantly

---

OLDER BROTHER DRIVING

Striking his head when he fell from a balky tractor, Gilbert Day Gardner, 6½, son of Mr. and Mrs. John C. Gardner of Putnam Settlement, was instantly killed at noon today.

The family explained that the boy was riding on a tractor driven by his older brother, John C. Jr., 11½, when it ran out of gas on a hill near the James Hume farm on the Creek Road.

The tractor began to jerk and buck and the smaller boy was thrown off, onto the roadway. He was rushed to Genesee Memorial Hospital, but Coroner Raymond L. Warn of Oakfield said that death had been instantaneous and that the boy was dead on arrival at the hospital. He was run over by the cultipacker which the tractor was hauling. The coroner said death was due to a fractured skull. State Police investigated.

The youngsters were en route from the Fred Gardner farm to their home when the accident occurred. The family said that John Jr., had been driving a tractor for two years and was well experienced in its operation.

H. E. Turner Mortuary handled the arrangements, as it would almost forty years later when the boy who had killed Gilbert killed himself. For those four decades Gardner lived with a guilt more crushing than any cultipacker; how could he not hate himself? "He's blamed himself all these years for what he couldn't possibly have prevented," said his mother, Priscilla, a year before John's death.

John Gardner's best short story, "Redemption," is laceratingly autobiographical. It begins:

> One day in April—a clear, blue day when there were crocuses in bloom—Jack Hawthorne ran over and killed his brother, David. Even at the last moment he could have prevented his brother's death by slamming on the tractor brakes, easily in reach for all the shortness of his legs; but he was unable to think, or, rather, thought unclearly, and so watched it happen, as he would again and again watch it happen in his mind, with nearly undiminished intensity and clarity, all his life. The younger brother was riding, as both of them knew he should not have been, on the cultipacker, a two-ton implement lumbering behind the tractor, crushing new-ploughed ground. Jack was twelve, his brother, David, seven. The scream came not from David, who never got a sound out, but from their five-year-old sister, who was riding on the fender of the tractor, looking back. When Jack turned to look, the huge iron wheels had reached his brother's pelvis. He kept driving, reacting as he would to a half-crushed farm animal, and imagining, in the same stab of thought, that perhaps his brother would survive. Blood poured from David's mouth.

John's shoulders buckled underneath the blame. "It's not your fault," spoken however truthfully, is cold comfort to a boy who has crushed his little brother's skull.

"Gilbert was the kind of kid who would never hold on," says Marge Cervone, a longtime family friend who once rode on the back of a motorcycle with John, Gilbert, and their dad on a 100-mile trip to Rock City Park. (Marge, who cofounded an NAACP chapter in Batavia in the 1960s, despite Batavia's almost complete absence of colored people, is locally famous for taking in delinquents: She quit the Gardners' Presbyterian Church over its high-hatting and still bears a grudge because it, like most houses of worship these days, locks its doors during unholy hours.)

So Gilbert was not the sort of six-year-old who ought to be allowed to ride on the hitch joining a tractor to a cultipacker. With the hindsight of half a century, and living in a different world, we might even assign a measure of negligence to the parents. (Why didn't they check the gas?)

John was distraught, beyond solace. He had killed his brother. How can such a sin, even if God and neighbors deem it an accident, ever be expiated? Shortly after the incident he wrote this poem.

MY BROTHER

In two feet water my brother would wade
He'd do it,
All knew it.
No wilder imp was ever made.
'Twas true!
God knew!
My little brother, sweet though wild
Was better far than any child.
With my small brother, Gilbert Day
Oh yes he lived the mischief way.
Every minute sweet and kind
My brother,
Ask mother.
Blessed *was* the tie that bind
One another
With my brother.
With a will he shot at work and play
Laughing, singing, always gay.
But once he laughed and played too far.
His jolly songs no longer are.

And you wonder why John Gardner drank himself insensible.

"I grew up with farmers," said Gardner in a son of toil mood. "I learned more from farmers than from professors."

Not that the farmers returned the compliment. In her invaluable history of Batavia, Ruth McEvoy, retired Richmond librarian, wrote of *The Sunlight*

Dialogues, "Critics found the book brilliant. Most local readers were not sure what the author was talking about." (The Richmond Library's copy of *The Sunlight Dialogues* is inscribed, "To Ruth, My favorite librarian, John Gardner, April 28, 1973.")

Gardner set two novels in Batavia. In *The Resurrection* (1966), his little-read first novel, a philosophy professor returns home to die. In *The Sunlight Dialogues* (1972), a native son given to Gardnerian disquisitions on order, law, and morality comes home, well, to die. Before his sun goes down, however, he engages Chief of Police Fred Clumly in a series of metaphysical colloquies in our queer old jail, a "brownstone and concrete imitation castle set back among dying elms and maple trees."

This is hardly naked autobiography, but the Hodges are nothing if not Gardnerian in their muck and strangeness. Barber Conable, son of another poetry-reciting dairy farmer, remembers, "My wife and I, after we had been in Batavia about three or four years, looked at each other and said, 'Somebody ought to write about these people.' And we were just astonished when *The Sunlight Dialogues* came out. Of course it really is a novel: he didn't make the most of the opportunities of fact there."

As if returning the unheard compliment, Gardner conceived of the Hodge paterfamilias in *The Sunlight Dialogues* as a positively Conablian figure. In an undated letter written when the novel in progress was called *The Devil Under the Stairs*, Gardner wrote: "There's this family of Hodges, in Western New York, which radiates from one grand old man, a Congressman of the old fashioned sort (my grandfather, really): good politician, good reader of poetry, good farmer, lawyer, father, etc."

Gardner can be read, in patches at least, as a regionalist, not only of Western New York but of Vermont (*October Light* is awash in autumnal Green Mountain color, its dialectic, not to mention dialect, poised between Ethan Allen and Norman Rockwell). He also wrote bewitchingly of the Endless Mountains of Pennsylvania in *Mickelsson's Ghosts*.

Gardner insisted that *The Sunlight Dialogues* "provides a fine comic history of Western New York and provides the means for a foreigner's understanding the peculiar attitudes of Western New York—attitudes significant, in my opinion, to the 'American experience' in general.'" If it took 673 pages to teach that New York City girl about apple-knockers, so be it.

Publication of *The Sunlight Dialogues* inspired numerous hilariously inaccurate stories which claimed that Batavians were reading the bestselling novel frontward and backward, matching up fictive characters with their flesh and blood counterparts. In fact, as Miss McEvoy said, no one here could make heads or tails of it. Rare indeed was the dogged reader who made it past "The Dialogue on Wood and Stone." Anyway, the town had slipped away from him. Gardner remarked to one reporter, "The city where I grew up has vanished from the face of the earth. My children will never see Batavia, N.Y., as I knew Batavia, N.Y. . . . Only a few buildings are there to remind us of what it was."

The book is dappled with Batavia names, not what you'd expect given Gardner's dismissal of "realistic fiction [in which] you keep mentioning local roads to prove you're in Detroit." But there they are: landmarks ranging from the New York State School for the Blind (irresistible as metaphor; it offers the finest vista in the city) to Doehler-Jarvis (where my grandfather worked between policing Batavia and selling papers at Marshall's News Store). He drops the names of the Veterans Hospital, Stroh's Flower Shop, Sylvania, the Richmond Library, and all the old streets—Bank, Ross, Jackson, Harvester, Oak, Ellicott, Washington—which are ominously eclipsed by the new: the thruway across whose Batavia entrance Tag Hodge, the Sunlight Man, painted the word *love*.

The real excitement came with the announcement that *The Sunlight Man*, a genuine Hollywood *movie*, was to be shot in Batavia starring Dustin Hoffman and his actorly tics. (Failing to make *The Sunlight Man*, Hoffman jumped the meteorological fence and won an Oscar for *Rain Man*.) The blacklisted Communist Jules Dassin, Melina Mercouri's husband and a man who "made some of the most entertainingly bad films of the sixties and seventies," in David Thomson's estimation, wrote a Batavia-centric script. But Dassin was staggering from his disastrous Black Power film *Up Tight*, and so *The Sunlight Man* quietly set.

What I like best in Gardner's Batavia books are the offhand Presbo swipes at Catholics. Fred Clumly's cemetery-side observation is a gem: "Used to be Catholics were beaten from the start in a place like Batavia, but Clive Paxton broke that. Now half the richest men in town are Catholics. Bought up all the fine old houses from the families that used to have the money—and pretty well wrecked them. Tear big holes in them for picture windows, cut the trees off the lawns, paint 'em red, that kind of thing. Not that I'm saying all Catholics are like that. Just the way these men happened to be."

Thus speaketh, perhaps, the first lady deacon of the First Presbyterian Church—*but not the goddam Chief of Police!*

Just as Sinclair Lewis had his "Sauk Centricities," which gave the ballast of verisimilitude to his Babbitts and Gunches, so is Gardner unmistakably a product of literate Presbyterian Batavia. His Batavia tics dot even the non-Batavia books. An IRS man speaks in a "desperately low-class Italian accent" to the hopelessly in arrears Mickelsson. Professor Agaard says of his son the monster in *Freddy's Book*: "When he was small we had a woman who took care of him, a Mrs. Knudsen. One of those hellfire fundamentalists. I'm afraid she put the fear of the Lord into him. The hellfire part's behind him now—we're Presbyterians." In *Nickel Mountain*, in the Utica train depot, "An angry voice shouted, 'Which car for Batavia?' " The voice is—must be—angry: The detail is telling.

The single best Batavia passage in Gardner comes early in *The Resurrection*, a "Christian novel," by Gardner's description, in which James Chandler, a professor of philosophy, returns to his hometown to die. "Batavia had been, in his day, a farmers' city," writes Gardner, "feedstores, farm-machinery places, a plow factory, the Massey-Harris plant," and for spice, Italians on the south side, across the New York Central Railroad tracks.

While Chandler is reluctant to gainsay Progress, he asserts that "it was *not* all right that the narrow old brick street was gone. It was good, but it was not all right. There was not a trace of the comfortable old country town, nothing. Or if that was too strong, there was nothing that didn't stand out like a death's head, a Victorian gable singing Memento Mori above a cheap, glossy storefront."

This was the Progress that Gardner, like all boys raised by the Greatest Generation, was taught to venerate, although the best of them did so uneasily, and with mounting reservations. We read in Gardner's sprawling valediction *Mickelsson's Ghosts*—so unfortunately set in a university, the all-purpose mausoleum of contemporary fiction—of "mighty Binghamton, blasted by the idiocy of Urban Renewal." Mighty Binghamton, mighty Auburn, mighty Batavia: how the mighty have fallen.

In *The Sunlight Dialogues*, Gardner wrote of two Batavians: "They talked then of politics, in the age-old style of Western New York farmers, arguing shades of a point of view no longer remembered, much less believed, in most of the world." The shades arguing these shades had a kindred spirit in James L. Page, the mad Vermont farmer of *October Light*, who was born on the Fourth of July and blasted his sister's television set "to hell, right back where it come from." The novel sets up my kind of political dichotomy: not the exhausted and inane liberal versus conservative, but rather Progressive versus Reactionary, as James's sister Sally believes in agribusiness, supermarkets, New York City, the Equal Rights Amendment, and nuclear power. That is to say, she believes in the destruction of rural America, and who can blame James for locking her up?

As a born and bred hick, no matter how many baguettes he ate at Bread Loaf, Gardner understood that city living dehumanizes: His corpulent good Samaritan Henry Soames in *Nickel Mountain* perceived that "a man could turn into an animal, then. It was something about living in the city, that was all he could figure."

The pretentiously surnamed Stephen Singular, writing in *The New York Times Magazine*, dismissed Gardner as a "rumpled gnome," a freak whose "white hair falls over his shoulders so he looks something like a pregnant woman trying to pass for a Hell's Angel." (A good line, that.) Gardner's real sin, however, was that, "like Tolstoy" (who also wrote an unreadable novel titled *The Resurrection*), he "has an anti-city bias (especially an anti–New York City bias)." The fact that that city's clerisy has an anti–apple-knocker bias is never worthy of mention.

"A very unpleasant, aggressive young man," Gardner called Singular in an interview in the *New Orleans Review*. Singular was a city boy, no doubt, a smug smarty-pants. "I think big cities like New York or Chicago tend to foster a certain cynicism that's different from a rural upbringing," said Gardner. Whether or not "the highest purpose of art is to make people good by choice," as Gardner wrote in *On Moral Fiction*, the disappearance of rural America (more of our countrymen are in prison than live on farms) makes a renaissance of Gardnerian moralism about as likely as an anti-Masonic restoration.

My favorite summary of Gardner's politics came from a 1977 interview in *The Atlantic*. "I am on the one hand a kind of New York State Republican, conservative," Gardner told his interlocutors. "On the other hand, I am a kind of bohemian type. I really don't obey the laws. I mean to, but if I am in a hurry and there is no parking here, I park."

This sort of communal anarchism, respectful of middle-class and town proprieties if not always observant of them, is perfectly fitted for Batavia—or at least the Batavia of my imagination.

Two months before his end, Gardner was profiled, sympathetically, by Curt Suplee in *The Washington Post*. They met in a bar "in the shadow of the Plaza" in what Edward Abbey called the Vampire City. By chat's end, "the martini count" approached double digits. Gardner, his "boyish face somewhere between Prince Valiant and Mickey Rooney," his "pudgy, grimy hand" greedily grasping the martini glass, slurred out a defense of

Mickelsson's Ghosts, boasted that he was "the spokesman for Middle America," and, sadly, recanted, in a sloshingly apologetic way, the innerving attacks he had launched on the Gods of the Moment in *On Moral Fiction*. "I thought those guys I don't like were not really liked by readers either," he told Suplee. "I thought it was just a New York establishment con." It was, John, it was! Apologize for nothing!

Through this alcoholic haze we ought not to lose sight of John Gardner the Good, the faithful son and reckless friend. Virtually every week for the last year of his life he made the 400-mile round trip between Binghamton and Batavia to care for his father, who had suffered a debilitating stroke. Instead of stuffing John Sr. in a nursing home, Gardner rode his trusty steed, a Harley-Davidson Electroglide 1200, to perform heroic acts that put the knights and ladies of his adolescent fantasies to shame. He planted crops, dressed his seventy-one-year-old father, helped him to the toilet, cooked for him and the weakening Priscilla, sturdied him to walk with the aid of a four-pronged cane, and read to him, especially from *Treasure Island* and E. Nesbitt's children's book *The Magic City*. This was Bud the Eagle Scout. Bud the serenader of the First Presbyterian Friendly Class. Bud the heaven-bound.

His fiancée at the time of his death, Susan Thornton, who wrote a memoir about their relationship titled *On Broken Glass: Loving and Losing John Gardner* (2000), told a small gathering at the University of Rochester that after their marriage, she and John were going to repatriate to Batavia. They planned to move in with the senior Gardners, helping around the farm while John played the role of the Great Man Revenant, perhaps teaching at Genesee Community College. (Marge Cervone, among others, believes that a colon cancer that had almost killed Gardner in the 1970s had recrudesced. Like Professor Chandler in his first novel, Professor Gardner was coming home to die.)

John Gardner never made it back to Batavia alive. On September 14, 1982, the same day Princess Grace descended to her new kingdom and four days before Gardner was to make his third "till death do we part" pledge (his marriage to Susan Thornton was to be at St. Paul's Episcopal Church in Rochester), Gardner's Harley failed to make a curve in Oakland Township in Susquehanna County, Pennsylvania. He was dealt a fell blow by the handlebars. (Pennsylvania roads are notoriously ill-maintained: he'd never have missed an easy curve closer to home, his real home.)

"The afternoon was balmy, bright; the roads were dry," explained his literary executor, Nicholas Delbanco. "He was a cautious and experienced driver, a few miles from home; he swerved—to avoid another vehicle, perhaps?—and fell. . . . It is clear he was trying to make it, fighting to survive."

This was not so clear to everyone. Gardner's younger brother, Jim, once speculated, in a speech at the Perry Public Library, that John's death may have been suicide, a logical suspicion given the ubiquity of dreams of self-annihilation in Gardner's fiction. Priscilla Gardner thought that "he must have blacked out or had a heart attack before the accident." Susan Thornton says that he was driving while impaired, if not drunk. In any event, H. E. Turner, the funeral home that embalmed the Sunlight Man after his death on September 13, 1966, did the same for its creator, who died sixteen years and one day later.

John Gardner's funeral was held at the First Presbyterian Church on Main Street, across from the post–Vatican II travesty of my St. Joe's. Four hundred mourners packed the church, most of them locals. The pallbearers were his brother and cousins, not Bill Gass, Stanley Elkins, and the rest of the legion of the walking unread. A cassette tape played John and his son Joel's duet on "Amazing Grace" with French horns, the instrument of deliverance for the boy who kills his brother in "Redemption." Ann Emmans played "The Old Rugged Cross" on the organ: "So I'll cherish the old rugged cross, / Till my trophies at last I lay down; / I will cling to the old rugged cross, / And exchange it some day for a crown." (Ann recalls this as the most hymn-filled service in the thirty-seven years she has played the organ at Presbyterian funerals. Most of the selections were Welsh, and the assembled Gardners and relatives sang in full throat—the way Italians might.)

In the December following John's death, First Presbyterian thespians put on *The Sam Weber's Toyshop Miracle*, a Christian-Jewish celebration of Christmas written by Gardner and his second wife, Liz Rosenberg. J. D. LeSeur starred as Mr. Weber the Jewish toymaker. Proceeds from the play helped buy the church a new Schlicker organ. When Priscilla Gardner died five years later, Ann Emmans would use it to pump out another funereal rendition of "The Old Rugged Cross." As she would in 1993, when father John finally followed his two eldest sons to the family plot.

John Gardner was buried next to Gilbert in the Grand View Cemetery on Batavia's outskirts, near Terry Hills golf course and about a nine-iron chip from the Protestant Kauffmans, the ones who never met Rosary-saying Irish Catholic girls. His epitaph is from his elegy for an artist friend, the poem "Nicholas Vergette 1923–1974." It reads, "ALL HE SPOKE OR CAST WAS MYSTERIOUS AND HOLY." (The verse goes on to castigate "the old stiff-minded gods" and the "unduly religious" and praise a deistic "spirit of God as sunlit pastures," all goldenrod and daisies, not a cultipacker in sight.)

"I think a writer who leaves his roots leaves any hope of writing importantly," said Gardner, and while he was seldom if ever tristful about the old home place, all weepy and adust about orange gloamings on the Putnam Road, he is back among us, for good, and despite what the Scripture says, he is not exactly without honor in his hometown.

5

Warren Hunting Smith

The Quintessential Genevan, 1993

Warren Hunting Smith, proudly clear-sighted. Collection of Bill Kauffman.

A handwritten note from Smith to the author. Collection of Bill Kauffman.

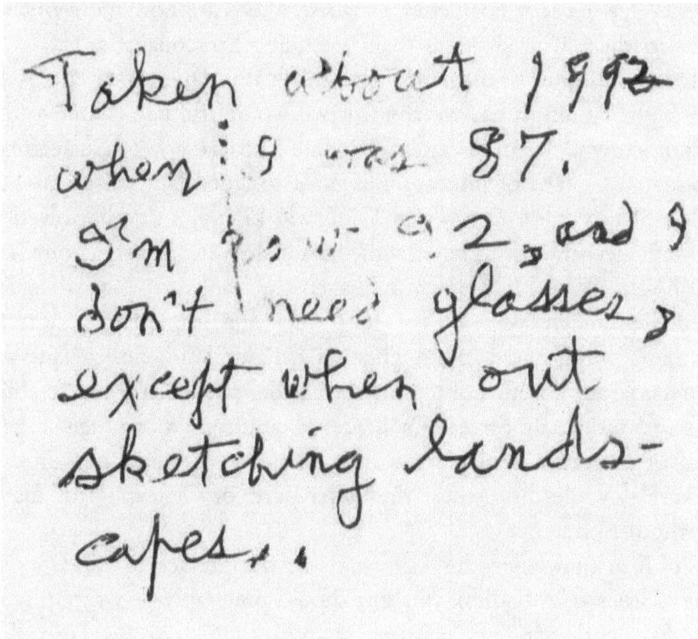
Taken about 1992 when I was 87. I'm now 92, and I don't need glasses, except when out sketching landscapes.

"To be merely queer is no achievement, but to be brilliantly individualistic is a fine art which Geneva brought to perfection." So declares Warren Hunting Smith in *The Misses Elliot of Geneva*, a delightful novel first published in 1940 and now reintroduced to Upstaters in *The Crooked Lake Review*.

I chatted with Mr. Smith recently in the summer house behind the grand brick Italianate in which he was raised on the family property on Castle Street in Geneva. Next door is the house in which his father was born; down Castle Street a ways is the observatory his granduncle constructed for William R. "Sky" Brooks, the Phelps village photographer and second most prolific comet discoverer (he found 27) in astronomical history.

Mr. Smith led a professional double life: He was both an editor of the Yale Edition of the Horace Walpole correspondence and a chronicler of old Geneva. Half his time was spent in Georgian England, the other half in the genteel Geneva of the prewar era. Never the twain shall meet? Not quite. The Pulteneys, who laid out Geneva, were denounced by Walpole.

Mr. Smith is the only man I've ever met whose favorite contemporary American novelist is Louis Auchincloss—"the one who deals with the world

I'm familiar with." That world is running down with the century; the WASP ascendency has passed. For better or worse, there are now more practicing Muslims in these United States than practicing Episcopalians.

To those of us who do not remember the America of the WASPs, Warren Hunting Smith has vouchsafed two wonderful books, one a history of his hometown, the other an affectionate satirical novel resurrecting the old Episcopal Geneva of impecunious razor-tongued lady aristocrats.

The history is *An Elegant but Salubrious Village*, a title borrowed from the early-nineteenth-century travel writer Elkanah Watson's verdict on Geneva. A local house, W. F. Humphrey, published the book in 1934, when Smith was but twenty-eight years of age. It is saucy and impudent, very much a young man's work, and a thoroughgoing delight. With nonchalant superciliousness, young Smith honors his own tribe, particularly the established families of South Main Street—"a citadel of culture in a commercial nation, a haven of leisure in a bustling world, an oasis of Southerners in a land of Yankees"—while dismissing "the uglier parts of Geneva"—for instance, the Methodist church.

Smith acknowledges his callowness in the preface to *An Elegant but Salubrious Village*: "A book of this sort should preferably be written by some mellow old gentleman, full of those memories which younger people can acquire only with painful research. Unfortunately, no such old gentleman has shown any literary interest in Geneva, so I have ventured to usurp the vacant place. . . . In fifty years more, perhaps, I shall be able to write a really thorough account of Geneva."

More thorough, perhaps, but surely not more entertaining. Mr. Smith writes as a witty young snob: "The very name 'Geneva, New York' is a sort of protective coloring, suggesting provincialism of the worst sort. We feel, when we hear it, as we do when we hear of someone named George Washington Schwartz or Michelangelo Snooks; it is as much a surprise to find real charm in this town with the pretentious foreign name as it would be to discover that Mr. Schwartz is really descended from the Washington family, or that Mr. Snooks is actually one of the Buonarroti."

Smith is properly proud of his hometown, which is "no cramped and provincial assembly of village lawyers and doctors." He doffs his hat westward to Canandaigua, the seat of Ontario County, only to give it the back of his hand. "Geneva," he writes, "unlike Canandaigua, never became a hotbed of lawyers. Indeed the distinctive Geneva profession, if any, has been that of doing nothing at all."

Well, not exactly nothing. True, the "old Geneva families . . . soiled their hands very little with business," but they had an enviable surety about them. The city's apotheosis is the gray-haired lady stepping down Main Street, head held high despite her threadbare clothes: "There is no fluttering hesitation in her manner, no false pretenses, no striving to keep up appearances. She knows that her family rank, her breeding, and her sharp tongue entitle her to a position from which she can look down on mere millionaires with disdain. She greets her friends cheerfully; puts incompetent shopgirls in their places ('I can see no excuse for stupidity!') and as she goes on her way, we realize that we have seen one of Geneva's choicest institutions—the Indigent Gentlewoman."

Indeed, the Indigent Gentlewoman rivaled Horace Walpole as the steady flame in Smith's professional life. Born into a city overrun with piquant old ladies, he has ever been under their spell. In the preface to his doctoral dissertation, *Architecture in English Fiction* (Yale University Press, 1934), Smith thanked "those dear sentimental ladies of eighteenth-century fiction, with whom I have 'kept company' for three pleasant years."

He soon found suitable replacements closer to home. For while in New Haven, Smith began work on what was to be his only published novel, *The Misses Elliot of Geneva*.

The Misses Elliot are "Primrose and Candida, names which had a somewhat virginal sound, appropriate to the one hundred and sixty-five years of celibacy which their two lives represented." They live near South Main Street, and from their cottage they hurl thunderbolts at "foreigners, Democrats, High Churchmen, and companies that didn't pay dividends." (And, as with all old ladies of whatever station, the "little bandits," whose doting aunts they most certainly are not.)

"There was something Olympian about their wrath," Smith writes; "they didn't scowl and sputter like cross old women, nor did they raise their voices to a cackle; they merely stood in majesty, filling the air with crackling sparks of invective." And woe unto those who cross Primrose's and Candida's paths. The sisters possess adamantine wills: they are given to walking out of Trinity Episcopalian church when they detect papist heresies. Stricken with scarlet fever, they ignore the quarantine and make their daily rounds, sending horrified friends scattering to safehouses.

Although Mr. Smith spent vacations and spare moments at the Castle Street house, he was domiciled in New Haven. A friend in that city read *The Misses Elliot* and passed the manuscript to an editor at Farrar & Rinehart, which purchased it on the recommendation of poet Stephen Vincent Benet, who wrote, "This is a genre piece but with a certain universal application. It hasn't any particular plot—it's just the story of two old-maid sisters and through them of a certain kind of individualistic American small-city society, independent, crotchety, brisk and always speaking its mind. It's slight, but I found it delightful."

Farrar & Rinehart brought the book out—in two printings—in 1940. Reviews were kind. In *The New York Times* Louise Maunsell Field called *The Misses Elliot* "very entertaining" and "gently humorous."

Yet because many of the characters—including the eponyms—had obvious real-life models, "it distressed some of the older inhabitants," Mr. Smith recalls.

"My family were not very enthusiastic. My father thought that it was a rather unkind book. They were preparing for a certain amount of flack. One old friend of the family said, 'I wonder why when somebody has written a very good book about Geneva he should turn around and write one that is most objectionable.' "

"I had one indignant letter from a nephew of the original Misses Elliot who said I held his aunts up to ridicule. Whereas one of his cousins told him, 'I don't think you have any right to write that. Cousin Virginia was just a hellion. She deserved everything she got.' " Mr. Smith—calling him "Warren," even on the homeliest page, seems an impertinence—laughs heartily.

"They were to some extent composites," the author says of his tart heroines, "but I didn't have to exaggerate their prejudices, which were very intense and very vocal. I merely sharpened their utterances."

The indignant Genevans were wrong, and Mr. Benet was right; this charming book is, in its irreverent way, deeply respectful of the sisters Elliot and their hometown. It's also chockablock with bons mots, for example, "Every old lady had to have either an old beau in the cemetery or a new one in the parlor, and preferably several of each."

Though the tone is light throughout, we know we are witnessing the last magnificent specimens of a dying breed. "They felt that the United States of America was, in a spiritual sense, almost their own property, just as they felt that Geneva almost belonged to them."

Edmund Wilson wrote of much the same feeling in his autumnal elegies *Upstate* and *The Cold War and the Income Tax*. The country really did, once, belong to those old WASPs, but it does no more, and all the former owners have left is their sting.

I have ancestors who chauffeured a couple of the great and not-so-great Upstate families, and from this end of the stick Mr. Smith's grand dames can look like withered cheapskates who put on ridiculous airs. Still, it's hard not to be a bit elegiac. Primrose is dead and Walmart sits athwart Geneva, and who is to say that progress is always benign?

Mr. Smith tried the novel again. He speaks warmly of one tale of a lady who believed that "the way to make a nursing home special was to have a centenarian as one of the inmates. The one she finally ended up with was an elderly black cook who had worked for one of the local families. I had a lot of fun with that but it didn't go over with the publisher, so I did nothing more about it."

Popular historian Carl Carmer pronounced Geneva "the most distinctive of upstate cities." Located above Seneca Lake, it was once known as the Charleston of the North. It had a southern feel, dotted by porticoed Greek Revival mansions built by the city's early aristocratic families, transplants from Maryland and Virginia.

The vigilance of local citizens, Mr. Smith among them, kept Geneva from the ruinous fate of so many small Upstate cities. The idiotic "slum clearance" program, which destroyed historic townhouses and brick tenements teeming with life and transferred slum dwellers to impersonal public housing concentration camps, swung the wrecker's ball in Geneva, but most of the city's notable commercial buildings and residences were saved.

My Batavia's midcentury decline can in some ways be traced to the sons and daughters of the established families, who fled for greener pastures and took with them a bedrock of civic responsibility. The same was true, to some extent, of Geneva, but the old ladies stayed (because they had nowhere else to go?) and it is due largely to stubborn pride that Geneva is still . . . well, Geneva.

"Poverty is a blessing to old Geneva ladies, though they themselves don't seem to think so," Smith wrote in *The Misses Elliot.* "It keeps them rooted to their native soil when other people are losing their local flavor abroad. It makes them keep the old-fashioned clothes and antique ornaments which seem almost a part of them. It gives them the chance to perform the little acts of grace which only poor old ladies know that other poor old ladies need."

Smith devoutly hoped in 1931 that "Geneva, with her unusual residential attractions, will never be transformed into that hideous monster, an American industrial center," and it wasn't, but his country's involvement in the Second World War just one decade later almost claimed Geneva as a municipal casualty. The Sampson naval training station, twelve miles to the city's south, loosed 45,000 young men on the old maids' paradise. The result was hardly edenic: Geneva went honky-tonk. Which would have been fine, if all it gave Geneva was a spicy fillip. Alas, the government remodeled many of the fine old homes into makeshift barracks, and the city took on ramshackle airs. Rochester newspaperman Arch Merrill, returning after an absence of twenty-six years, wrote, "I hardly recognized the old town. It was like seeing your dignified maiden aunt toss aside her prayer book and pince nez and swing into a strip tease."

Perhaps it is best that Primrose and Candida never lived to see that.

Mr. Smith is a kindly man and a gracious employer, say his nurses. And he is—as we all are—very much a product of his upbringing. I ask him if he shares the Elliots' prejudices. "Having grown up in that atmosphere, to some extent I can't help sharing it, but I'm much more open-minded than I think my parents were. I remember my father being quite distressed to hear that I was taking out in New Haven a girl with some foreign name." I love the way he says "foreign"; like John Houseman hissing "they ehn it" in those classic Smith Barney commercials.

I ask him if the old families still dominate Geneva politics. No, he says, the current officials "are not the well-known people at all; they are apt to be shopkeepers and dealers and people like that."

He smilingly recalls Mr. Chew, the leading banker of bygone years. "He said, 'Geneva is a city of homes and a few stores and that's enough. We don't want factories, they bring foreigners, and we don't like that.' The Chamber of Commerce would disapprove of him heartily." Mr. Smith chuckles, in a tone that suggests he's not paid his Chamber dues in many a year.

Mr. Smith wrote in *The Misses Elliot* of old Genevans: "They didn't have much money, but in Geneva that doesn't matter." Indeed, the novel and *An Elegant but Salubrious Village* drip with disdain for parvenus. But while the social wall between the old families and the new money still exists, the barrier is crumbling. "I remember there were people who moved down to Main Street who owned a sauerkraut factory and were very much looked down upon by the families around them. But I think nowadays anybody with a good deal of money, if, shall we say, civic-minded, would be accepted."

Did he ever dabble in politics? He is aghast. "Oh no, I never had anything to do with politics. Somebody suggested once that since I had independent means I ought to go into politics because I would be above the more ambitious average politicians, but of course a retiring scholar like me would be the worst person to try anything like that!"

While working on the Walpole edition Mr. Smith published *Hobart and William Smith: The History of Two Colleges* (Hobart and William Smith, 1972). His connection to the latter, a women's school, is familial: grand-uncle William Smith, one of three brothers who founded a prosperous tree nursery in 1846, endowed the college that bears his name with a gift of half a million dollars in 1908. (I was taken aback when I found not a single Horace Walpole reference in *Hobart and William Smith*.)

William Smith comes off as a vivid eccentric in his grandnephew's account. He was a bachelor, a spiritualist, and a man sometimes called a misogynist who nevertheless was befriended by the daughter of fervid abolitionist Gerrit Smith (he who bought John Brown's guns) and was encouraged by her to found a college for women.

William was no dabbler in spiritualism; he was a true believer. He visited the colony at Lily Dale, where no one ever dies, and his descendant still possesses a notebook of William's "filled with letters beginning 'Dear Mr. Smith,' and signed by such names as Socrates, Julius Caesar, and 'your loving aunt, Sally Coleman.' " He toyed with establishing a spiritualist school before settling on William Smith College.

"Oh yes, I remember Uncle William," says Mr. Smith. "I'm probably the last person who can remember him since he didn't circulate in Geneva society and wasn't interested in children."

"One reason Uncle William never put up a gravestone to his mother was that since he was corresponding with her through the spirit world, he wasn't particularly interested in her mortal remains." (Mr. Smith, no spiritualist, put up a tombstone in the old Washington Street Cemetery a couple of years ago.)

Warren Hunting Smith retains a tie with Hobart and William Smith; the new library bears his name. The school itself, however, while the city's largest employer, is less and less a part of the life of Geneva. "The people of the college have little interest in civic affairs," concedes Mr. Smith.

(Besides Warren Hunting Smith, two other estimable New York writers have Hobart connections: Phelps's Bellamy Partridge of *Country Lawyer* fame and the late Frederick Exley, author of *A Fan's Notes*, who fled the cold for the University of Southern California, only to return to drink himself to death amid his beloved Thousand Islands.)

I launch into one of my favorite routines, about how Mr. Smith's was the last generation of Upstate men of letters. I read the roll call: Walter D. Edmonds, Henry W. Clune, Carl Carmer, Samuel Hopkins Adams. Do you feel any kinship with them? I burble.

"No, none whatever I should say."

Well, did you ever read them?

"No, I never read them."

This is not unexpected: Smith is a Genevan through and through, less so an Upstater. As a regional writer he is best classed with William Kennedy, whose Albany, like Geneva, contrasts starkly with its purlieus.

I ask him what I always ask eminent old writers: Do you ever go back and read your stuff?

"No, I seldom read them. Sometimes favorite passages. I'm sometimes delighted to find that I wrote as well as I did." He does not say this immodestly, just as a matter of fact.

He may not communicate with the dead, but Mr. Smith is given to an admirable filiopietism. He edited the letters of his cousin Adele Mali (Geneva Historical Society, 1979) on the centennial of her birth, and he seems the sort who always knows what the nieces and nephews are up to.

The homestead is now more a museum than a home, filled as it is with the furniture and artwork and gewgaws of a century and a half of Smiths. The family divested itself of the nursery business in the 1950s. Mr. Smith wrapped up the Walpole edition in 1982 with a five-volume index—"without a computer," he notes with pride.

Warren Hunting Smith turned eighty-seven in October. He admits to "excellent" general health, though a series of ailments has confined him largely to chair and bed. "My walking is pretty shaky, and it takes two people to hoist me to my feet," he says, but he still perambulates about the flowery family grounds.

And he paints. His most recent book, *Gentle Enthusiasts in Art* (Geneva Historical Society, 1986), honored the Sunday painters and amateur artists and sketching parties of his youth. In the Misses Elliots' day Geneva had been "a town where nearly everyone could at least sketch," and Mr. Smith, for one, does to this day.

He also still attends, when he can, Trinity Church, worship house of the Elliots, towering Gothic redoubt of old Episcopal Geneva. When all is ashes and embers, Trinity Church will no doubt be left standing.

Only one close relative, a nephew, lives in Geneva. (There are cousins.) Most of the old ladies have fulfilled the prophecies of the actuaries. The Misses Elliots' "many-gabled cottage" was torn down long ago. "The site is an access area now to a college property," says Mr. Smith. "It has a walk across it and some ornamental planting." Better than a parking lot.

In a series of sketches titled *Originals Abroad* (Yale University Press, 1952), Smith wrote that his subjects "were not important people, to their contemporaries or to us; their lives were not exemplary. They were not the builders of the British Empire but merely citizens who went forth as witnesses to the infinite variety of the national individuality and character; Britain's reputation for vigor and originality came from the careers of just such spirited (if wayward) characters as these."

So, too, for Geneva. Whatever her current fortunes—and this bosky lakeside city of residences looks pretty damn good to a child of Upstate's Dresden—Geneva, at its acme, its brilliantly individualistic golden age, is preserved for us in the works of Warren Hunting Smith.

In a region in which "she's different" is the supreme put-down, Mr. Smith is our witty champion of idiosyncrasy. "Even the obscurest Genevans are somehow distinguished, and know how to live like individuals and not like a flock of sheep," he wrote six decades ago. In word and deed, Warren Hunting Smith is the quintessential Genevan.

6

Tim Tielman

The Buffalo Saver, 2017

Tim Tielman, saving Buffalo. Courtesy of Tim Tielman.

My wife and I celebrated our thirtieth wedding anniversary in a mental hospital. I drove her there, I admit. But hey, she asked for it.

We were not patients thereof but rather imbibers in the bar of the new Hotel Henry, which is embedded in the erstwhile Buffalo State Asylum for the Insane (1880), a massive and portentous cluster of eleven buildings designed by H. H. Richardson, eponym of the Richardsonian Romanesque architectural style. Constructed of locally mined Medina sandstone, surmounted by two great Gothic towers, its grounds landscaped by Frederick Law Olmsted and Calvert Vaux (whose lesser works include Central Park at the state's hind end), the asylum disgorged its last patient forty years ago.

By the 1990s, Richardson's creation had fallen into a state of disrepair bordering on the immedicable. That any structures at all, let alone a masterpiece on its way to restoration, exist on this spot today owes to the labor and love of many people, but not one is more passionate, more eloquent, or more Buffalonian than Tim Tielman.

I met Tim in 2003, when his Campaign for Greater Buffalo History, Architecture, and Culture sponsored a talk upon the release of my *Dispatches from the Muckdog Gazette*. (There I also met Beverly Felser, who had defeated my mother in the 1957 Elba Onion Queen contest. Mom always claimed that Beverly made eyes at the judges, a scurrilous charge the winner strenuously denied.)

Tim made an immediate impression. A witty and gritty and irreverent historic preservationist who loved the Old Weird Buffalo yet had command of the tedious minutiae of planning policy? A charismatic urban geographer? What gives?

He was then in the midst of a metamorphosis. Once damned as an obstructionist, a spoilsport throwing dead cats in the basilica of the American religion of capital-*P* Progress, Tielman was on his way to being hailed as prescient, perspicacious, a public treasure. Donn Esmonde, longtime *Buffalo News* columnist, wrote in 2013 of the "transformation" of Tim Tielman: "Once maligned and marginalized by the powers that be, Tielman now is used as a civic spokesman. Not since Linda Blair's head swiveled in *The Exorcist* have we seen as dramatic a turnaround."

The *enfant terrible* has become an *eminence grise*.

I spoke recently with Tim on the front porch of the 1906 Period Revival home he shares with his wife Suzanne on a small leafy street in a Buffalo that is the antipode of the city mockingly poetized by Vachel Lindsay:

Within the town of Buffalo
Are prosy men with leaden eyes.
Like ants they worry to and fro,
(Important men, in Buffalo.)

Tielman's Buffalo—the real Buffalo—is a city of neighborhoods, even if some of them were sliced and diced and almost eradicated by urban renewers and highwaymen—the prosy men with leaden eyes of the 1950s and '60s.

Nineteenth-century Buffalo, boomed by the Erie Canal, had flourished as a prosperous entrepot between the Great Lakes and New York City. Olmsted, who designed its network of parks and parkways, called it "the best planned city in America, if not the world." By 1900, Buffalo was the nation's tenth most populous city. A year later it hosted the Pan-American Exposition, where Leon Czolgosz assassinated President McKinley, thereby inflicting Teddy Roosevelt on the country.

Though a shot-and-a-beer steel town in the twentieth-century public imagination, Buffalo was also a city of architectural gems: It and Chicago are the only cities to boast works by the American trinity of H. H. Richardson, Louis Sullivan, and Frank Lloyd Wright.

Yet its population has collapsed from 580,000 in 1950 to about 250,000 today, even as its county of Erie has hovered around the 900,000 mark. Tim Tielman explains:

"In the span of one generation—from 1957 to 1980—downtown Buffalo, New York was transformed from a cluster of thousands of commercial establishments and homes, the central place of an eight-county hinterland, into a far less populous commercial desert devoid of most central place functions. The physical transformation was deliberate and methodical, driven by downtown elites, enabled by federal and state programs that were tapped by a political-bureaucratic apparatus eager for easy money. All saw the traditional city as threatening and obsolete. The apparatus measured its success by the degree to which the physical form of the city was changed. Architects and media joined in to create a self-romanticizing coterie bent on heroic action."

Well, who better to fight a self-romanticizing coterie bent on destruction than another self-romanticizing coterie whose motive is love of the city?

Tim Tielman, like any patriot, grew up loving his place, yet loathing—and learning from—the appalling things that had been done to it. He is the son of immigrant parents: a Dutch mother and a Dutch Indonesian father who migrated to Maryland, where Tim's dad worked for a US

Department of Agriculture program designed, Tim says, "to teach benighted Europeans enlightened American agricultural techniques: get big or get out, and please buy an American tractor on credit!"

They shuffled off to Buffalo when dad took a job in a chemical factory. Tim was born in 1959, when the family resided in a now-demolished public housing project. The family of ten struggled financially, and when Tim was twelve they repatriated to the Netherlands. He hated the four-year exile—"I was all-American, loved baseball"—and upon turning sixteen he bought a plane ticket to Buffalo with earnings from odd jobs.

Here his story takes on a hipster Horatio Alger tinge. Heeding his mother's advice, Tim asked a priest at St. Joseph's Roman Catholic Church on Main Street if he might board with a parish family. He was delivered to the not-so-tender mercies of a "stark raving nuts" nun, from whose custody he quickly escaped. The plucky lad found a job in a downtown bookstore, sublet an apartment, got his GED, and wound up studying geography at SUNY College at Geneseo.

In best autodidact fashion, freshman Tielman read through every back issue of *Architectural Forum* magazine in the Geneseo library basement. And he noticed something: "When I would go back to Buffalo and see them demolishing everything to create a Great New City, I said wait a minute: the Netherlands is pretty advanced economically and they're doing okay in buildings that are 500 years old and in cities that a 12-year-old can get around in, by bike or tram. Buffalo's going about this the wrong way."

It was a wrong turn that almost every midsized American city had taken in the postwar madness. In Buffalo, a series of federally funded urban renewal and highway construction projects, beginning in the 1950s, displaced more than 10,000 people and demolished over 1,000 businesses. Houses and shops were expropriated; expressways bisected, which is to say destroyed, neighborhoods, or at least those neighborhoods whose residents were not prominent in the Chamber of Commerce. As Tielman says, "Highway construction was always the partner of urban renewal. Get an atlas of any city in the US, look at the road projects in the 1960s, and overlay a map of socioeconomic factors: income, education, race—the highway is going through."

As the wrecking ball swung, one of the most resonant voices of protest belonged to African American architectural pioneer Robert T. Coles, son of a Buffalo postal worker. Coles pled, unsuccessfully, for preservation, for neighborhood, for the little shops, china cups, and virginity—no, wait; that was the Kinks in "Village Green Preservation Society"—and against urban renewal, wanton destruction, and the regime of automobile *uber alles.* In 1963 Coles wrote: "We are mistaking newness for goodness. . . . [I]n wandering through the downtown neighborhoods, one sees so much that could be saved; one wonders whether it might be better for Buffalo to rehabilitate what it already has to attract its former residents back into the city rather than to build at tremendous cost new towers in the horizon in the midst of blight and deterioration."

But what did a young native son architect, product of Buffalo's schools and Buffalo's streets, know? Especially when starchitects like Minoru Yamasaki (One M&T Plaza; he also designed the infamous Pruitt-Igoe housing project in St. Louis) and Manhattan's Harrison & Abramovitz (Main Place Tower), with their soulless modernist skyscrapers, were teaching the city fathers how to raze what Buffalo was and raise a new, clean, rational, and brutalist city? (Those 1960s architects were right out of the Robert Frost poem: "With him the love of country means / Blowing it all to smithereens / And having it all made over new.")

Urban renewal was the lethal marriage of progressive urban engineering with what Tim calls the "kakistocracy"—thieves who justify their crimes against place in the canting and condescending language of efficiency and inevitability.

Senator Pat Moynihan once said, while being driven through urban-renewal-decimated Auburn, New York, "In the 1950s, with a progressive government and newspaper, you got into urban renewal and destroyed everything of value in your town. If you'd had a reactionary newspaper and a grumpy mayor, you might still have it." Try to imagine Chuck Schumer or Kirsten Gillibrand saying something one–ten thousandth as perceptive. (Confirming Moynihan, the largest American city to reject urban renewal funding was Salt Lake City, whose voters, following the lead of their delightfully cranky libertarian Mayor J. Bracken Lee, rejected the federal bulldozer in 1965 by a vote of 29,119 to 4,900.)

Moynihan had a soft spot for Buffalo, probably because it was filled with the ethnic Catholics who claimed his heart, if not always his head. His support was critical in saving Louis Sullivan's terra-cotta–ornamented Guaranty Building (1896) from senseless demolition. (In a 1961 essay in *Commentary*, Moynihan called Buffalo "a big, ugly, turbulent city." I once asked him if that description caused any problems in his campaigns. He looked at me incredulously. "How many people in Buffalo do you think read *Commentary*?")

"Absent the federal and state money, none of this devastation occurs in Buffalo or Niagara Falls," Tielman says, adding, "Where did this free money go? To the existing power structure"—whose acts of destruction were facilitated, I regret to say, by urban Catholic mayors, who sacrificed significant portions of their cities to the Greatest Generation's Greatest God: Progress.

Tim Tielman began speaking and writing in praise of what he calls "paleo-urbanism" in the mid-1980s. He was, at first, a gadfly—"the urban design book-pusher of Buffalo," he laughs—protesting the seemingly limitless ways by which developers and politicians proposed to "improve" Buffalo by maiming, molesting, or extirpating the common inheritance. Whether a Frederick Law Olmsted park or a corner butcher shop, nothing was safe from the powerful men armed with plans and free federal money. Tim also enfiladed them with *Sharp Comix*, a satirical bimonthly, which provoked a $30 million lawsuit—"we settled for $100"—by the Trumpian Buffalo developer Carl Paladino.

After one event, Tim met Susan McCartney, cofounder of the Preservation Coalition of Erie County, which Tim would serve as executive director before leaving in 2002 to found the Campaign for Greater Buffalo History, Architecture, and Culture. Tim and Sue wed, they defended their cultural patrimony, and they divorced. But their progeny include not only two children but numerous once-threatened buildings now upright and thriving, obscure gems illumined, even baseball games played in a proper setting. The much-praised design of the downtown Coca-Cola—née Pilot—Field (1988), one of the earliest of the retro ballparks, is partly due to preservationist pressure to keep the stadium from being domed or otherwise denatured.

In the case of H. H. Richardson's asylum, the Preservation Coalition sponsored tours of the grounds in all their dilapidated splendor and promoted educational efforts to acquaint Buffalonians with this fading hulk of their heritage. It urged local officials to do basic maintenance on the state-owned landmark, but to no avail: The National Trust for Historic Preservation put the complex on its most endangered list.

As a last resort—a legal Hail Mary—the Coalition sued the state, arguing that Albany was statutorily obligated to maintain its designated historic buildings. In 2002 the New York Supreme Court concurred. The prospect of the state footing the bill for the legion of vacant psychiatric centers, courthouses, jails, waterworks, and suchlike under its ownership convinced Governor George Pataki to make a deal: If the cash-strapped Preservation Coalition would agree not to contest the state's appeal (it couldn't afford to anyway), the state would send $100 million to Buffalo for preservation of the Richardson asylum and the Frank Lloyd Wright–designed Darwin Martin House. Fifteen years later, the Martin House is a jewel and H. H. Richardson's alternative to Bedlam has returned from the moribund.

Yes, I know, this is taxpayers' money. Tim describes himself as a "liberal," though I'd call him a civic-minded localist. Regardless, the monuments and handiwork of our forbears deserve preservation, even reinvigoration, and besides, the first two tenants to open in the 463,000-square-foot Richardson-Olmsted Complex, the 100 Acres Kitchen and the 88-room Hotel Henry, are privately owned.

Tielman quickly learned that the best way to parry the "obstructionist" charge was to "always have a counterplan, an alternative path."

Sometimes, though, the kakistocrats and Bold Dreamers concoct plans so outrageously profligate and stupefyingly wrongheaded that obstruction becomes a bounden duty.

For instance, in the early years of this century local officials sought to lure Bass Pro, the big-box sporting-goods store, to anchor the development of Buffalo's Canal District, western terminus of the Erie Canal. The Canal District was a bustling tenderloin in the days when mules named Sal trudged the towpath; later it was pulverized and paved, a victim of urban renewal, a sacrifice to the parking lot Baal. Today, after excavation and restoration prompted by a Tielman lawsuit, "Canalside" is a popular site for recreation, concerts, and festivals.

But before this rebirth, the economic development boys had the bright idea of luring Bass Pro with a $35 million subsidy. The corporate giant took the bait. Politicians lined up for photo ops.

So the Campaign for Greater Buffalo went big-box hunting. It assembled a coalition including VOICE-Buffalo, a religious-social justice organization; the Sierra Club; and taxpayer watchdog Jim Ostrowski, son of South Buffalo (and of a New York State Supreme Court justice), attorney, and libertarian activist.

Among the most eloquent critics was Mark Goldman, restaurateur and historian, who has chronicled the destruction and incipient revivification of his adopted city in such books as *City on the Edge* (2007). Goldman said of Bass Pro:

> There's nothing good about it. It's bad public policy, bad economics, and bad governance. Bad public policy because subsidies to private companies do not, and cannot work. Bad

> economics because the project focuses on increasing supply and not demand; bad governance because it sends a terrible message to any others interested in doing business that we do not have a level playing field here . . . that there are a certain chosen few who get the benefits while the rest do not. The deal is rotten from the head down.

The left-right coalition sunk Bass Pro—which in hindsight even the magic bullet subsidize-anything-that-moves crowd admits was for the best. Says the libertarian Ostrowski: "Tim is a brilliant guy who knows the history of Buffalo down to the smallest detail. He used to be marginalized by the powers that be as is their usual reaction to real talent. However, they listened to him on Bass Pro and the waterfront is much better for it." But the Canal District is now threatened by every parent's nightmare: a *children's museum*, a $27 million project, jointly funded by a state development corporation and corporate donors, with the city offering a $1-a-year lease for forty years.

Tim is not enthused. "Did you know Buffalo is the largest city in the country without a children's museum?" he asks in mock outrage. "We can't let that stand!"

More seriously, he notes that "children's museums attract fewer people than cemeteries," and that this one "has nothing to do with the Canal District—it could be anywhere." What a condign caption for so many of the edifices that deface our cities: *This could be anywhere.*

Tielman envisions Canalside as more than just a place to drink craft beer and listen to Goo-Goo Dolls covers, let alone spend an excruciating hour at manufactured "play." He has proposed, and the powers that be are considering, a plan to open the Canal District to small buildings, shops, apartments, and commercial spaces. "We can rebuild a sustainable neighborhood where Buffalo started," says Tim, donning prophet robes, "and it can restart from this site following a philosophy based on historic preservation and what works urbanistically."

Jane Jacobs occupies the catbird seat on Tim's bookshelf. He rhapsodizes Jacobsian over pre–urban renewal Buffalo, which was "dense with buildings and crowded sidewalks, where one could wander block upon block, past shop after shop, restaurant after restaurant, office building after hotel, without apparent end. Buffalo was a beehive, where all of life's necessities, pleasures, and luxuries could be had within the square mile of its core."

Its demolition was not the work of some invisible hand or inscrutable force but rather, in Tielman's phrase, "social engineers" who destroyed the essence of the city. But maybe everything that dies someday comes back.

This is no woolgathering fantasy. For one of Tielman's greatest hits is Larkin Square, centerpiece of a once-abandoned industrial district, which Chris Hawley, senior planner for the City of Buffalo, calls "one of the true Rust Belt success stories."

The Larkin Company was a soap manufactory and mail order business associated with Elbert Hubbard, the eccentric apostle of the arts and crafts movement, and Frank Lloyd Wright, who designed a home for Larkin secretary Darwin Martin as well as the Larkin Administration Building (1906), generally considered a masterpiece of modern industrial architecture. (I leave aside the question of whether *that's* a good thing.)

In time, the Larkin Company went the way of all mortal things, especially mail order firms. A younger Larkin had defaced the building, over Wright's objections, with his own "improvements," and by the mid-1940s it was seized for unpaid taxes by the City of Buffalo. Purchase offers from a brewer and other dreamers were rejected, and in 1950 it was felled to make room for a proposed truck terminal that never came to be. Instead, Wright's Emersonian cathedral to "the ideal of virtuous work," as art historian Jack Quinan called it, was replaced by . . . a parking lot.

We parked in that lot as we visited Larkin Square, a bustling urban space hosting a 1930s service station converted to a restaurant, a vintage diner, a peaceful army of food trucks, an outdoor concert venue, a historically themed mini-golf course, and people-watching chairs to fit all shapes and sizes. Howard Zemsky, a preservation-minded developer and Russer Foods heir, has worked with Tielman and others to rejuvenate the once-desolate Larkinville district surrounding the square; the whilom postindustrial wasteland now houses the excellent Flying Bison Brewing Company, various design and architecture firms, and a burgeoning retail, manufacturing, and warehouse center. With its hanging perpendicular signage, awnings, and gooseneck lighting, Larkinville fairly sings "New Urbanism was here." Signally, the Congress for the New Urbanism held its 2014 national conference in resurgent Buffalo.

"Success, for me, is if someone can buy a quart of milk or get breakfast in the neighborhood," says Tielman, who describes Larkinville as a "free market urban environment" whose future he does not presume to predict. "You break up a big forbidding scale and allow smaller things to happen," he says. "You create the basic setting and then you let other people do what they can do."

Next time you're in Buffalo—and you really ought to visit; the Buffalos and Lowells and Pittsburghs are so much better for the soul than Orlando or Myrtle Beach—take one of the Campaign for Greater Buffalo's open-air bus tours. Drop by Larkin Square and Canalside. Visit the reified visions of Richardson, Sullivan, and Wright, and enjoy the vernacular architecture of local builders. These have been saved, or resurrected, by local patriots, men and women of all pedigrees, from South Buffalo Irish to Dutch Indonesian. What they did here, you and I can do in our own places, if we will but look, listen, and love.

7

Greg & Jackie & RaeAnn & Richard

Waitin' on a Friend, 2023

RaeAnn and Richard, being neighborly. Courtesy of RaeAnn Engler and Richard Beatty.

Friendship is "love without his wings," aphorized the flighty Lord Byron, but for feathery gnomes I prefer alt-country singer Robbie Fulks: "Wouldn't we all have wings / If God loved goodbyes?" (Fulks is an atheist, but we'll let that pass.)

Over the last few months I've witnessed a lesson in the virtues of winglessness nearly every morning at Pub Coffee Hub, nestled in the quondam Massey-Harris factory across from the Historic Batavia Cemetery on Harvester Avenue.

As I sip my latte—yeah, I know, stuff me in a garbage can filled with Bud Lights—and search fruitlessly for the *bon*, or at least *moyenne*, *mot*, I keep a clouded eye on the convivial quartet two tables to my left. Their fellowship was the product of happenstance happily delimited by place, and its recent reduction to a trinity has emphasized its strength.

The fixtures at this coffeehouse table are: Richard, genial laid-back music buff and chatty septuagenarian hippie, a native Floridian (same high school as Ron DeSantis, he says with an eyeroll); his wife RaeAnn, a past Batavia Homeowner of the Year, a woman whose voluntaristic energies propel a whole range of projects, from the community garden to the county arts agency—and as a girl she occasionally ate chipped beef on toast with Christian Laettner; and Ron, a retired social studies teacher, instructor in Catholic confirmation classes, and discerning tourist of America's baseball stadia. (He shares my queasiness over Dodger Stadium, built on the ruins of a Mexican-American neighborhood bulldozed for the sake of modernist architects.)

The fourth member of the quartet, Greg, is now in absentia, and barring a miracle will be from here on out.

He is a retired Methodist pastor, adjunct professor, and a scholar of his denomination who has published significant primary-source-heavy books with Emeth Press on nineteenth-century camp meetings and circuit riders.

Greg has a smart and gentle humor and capacious spirit. I'll bet he was a helluva good minister. Greg and his wife, Jackie, who of late has given shape and substance and a heavenly glow to the "for worse" parts of the marriage vow, had lived the mildly peripatetic life of a pastor's family until settling in Batavia a dozen or so years ago.

The dramatis personae met at a now-defunct coffee shop a dozen years ago. Woody Allen was righter than he knew when he said that 80 percent of life is showing up. There is a value to just being there. You become part of the daily landscape of the others who show up.

Richard recalls: "I would come into Coffee Culture every day. Greg would be sitting in a bench seat with a pile of papers and books. He wrote on napkins. Incredibly small handwriting. I would pass by and say, 'Good morning.' One morning I stopped and asked, 'What are you doing?' "

That's how friendship starts.

After Coffee Culture closed, their daily conversations carried over to Moon Java, as Pub Coffee Hub was first known. (Greg knew he'd love it when he learned that it had no Wi-Fi. He has praiseworthy Luddite tendencies.)

A minister and Christian intellectual is likely to touch on religious topics now and then, and Greg did, but "it was never a bone of contention," says Richard, who if not the village atheist is at least the village irreverent. They talked of God now and then, but Greg never persuaded Richard to profess and Richard never urged Greg to apostatize.

As for politics, they—like most Americans who keep a healthy distance from organs of propaganda—have no hunger for war. (Greg and Jackie were active in the peace movement of the 1960s.) They disagree, says Richard, about—well, how shall we phrase these issues with a bloodless neutrality?—sexual expression, reproductive law, and the legality of psychoactive substances. Richard is no rake, mind you, but he hates to see a joint go to waste.

It doesn't matter. No one at that table hides his or her opinions, but because they have come to know each other through their daily exchanges as rounded, multidimensional people rather than cardboard cutouts, honest and respectful—if sometimes chaffing and amused—disagreement is always the special of the day.

"Richard gets along with everyone," says RaeAnn. "He downplays the importance of their differences" and meets others on the vast common ground that most of us share. Which only shows that he is a man of his place: A 2019 study for *The Atlantic* found rural New York counties among the most "politically open-minded" jurisdictions in America.

When I see Richard and RaeAnn—who were president and treasurer, respectively, of our county's Green Party—talking and laughing and enjoying warm sodality with friends and potential friends regardless of the trivial matter of how they cast their meaningless votes, I think: This is how it should be, and this is how it is, still, in many places.

In the latter part of 2022, Greg began showing up at Pub Coffee Hub pushing a walker. Parkinson's had hit him, and hard. Soon he needed a friendly hoist to stand, and eventually it became a multifriend and multiminute project to get him to his feet, out the door, and into Jackie's Caravan.

Like most folks with debilitating conditions, Greg does not want to be treated as an object of pity. Understanding this, Richard kept up the love-disguised-as-insults male patter. "Hurry up, will ya, you're holding us up," Richard would hiss as Greg struggled to rise, or he would softly sing a snatch from the Rolling Stones: "I'm not waiting on a lady / I'm just waitin' on a friend."

On his and RaeAnn's regular visits to Greg during his hospitalizations, Richard would greet him as if they were standing along Bob Dylan's watchtower: "There must be some way outta here / Said the joker to the thief."

As the writing on the wall became clearer, Greg started giving things away. This included his extensive LP record collection, which is heavy on traditional Scottish and Irish songs and American and Canadian folk. (Surely no one has ever owned this many Ian & Sylvia records.)

At Greg's urging, Richard took 150 of his albums. Although Richard's tastes run more to outlaw/alternative (Townes Van Zandt, Jeffrey Lewis, Gurf Morlix), he has, at this writing, listened to a different one of Greg's albums for fifty-three consecutive days. (Today's turntable featured *Saved*, from Bob Dylan's Christian evangelist period.) When I say Richard listens to these records, I mean he *listens*. And he reads the liner notes. By now he must know more about the 1970s Scottish folkies Silly Wizard than any non–haggis eater in the world.

During the period when bad was giving way to worse, Greg labored over his next book: a daily devotional for ministers consisting of excerpts from the sermons of his beloved eighteenth- and nineteenth-century Methodist circuit riders. He made it to Day 295 (October 22) before Parkinson's stilled his pen.

Richard's album listening, however, continues. It is as if he is picking up and extending the daily devotional on a parallel track. His is an exercise in empathy, in forging a connection through which the barriers of time and illness disappear.

Will the circle be unbroken?

Greg is not at the table anymore, though Richard, RaeAnn, and Ron visit him and Jackie at their home. Jo Anna, another faithful friend, bakes for them. RaeAnn weeds Jackie's flower garden. When I mutter some inane observation—"Gee, that's nice of you"—RaeAnn, who seems to spend most of her busy hours performing acts of mercy and kindness for others, shrugs, saying, "Isn't that what friends are for?"

No, don't worry: She's not quoting the saccharine Dionne Warwick song. It's the title of a tune by the leftist Canadian Christian folksinger Bruce Cockburn, whom Richard has seen perform thirty-plus times.

In the final weeks of Greg's physical presence at Pub Coffee Hub, he learned that Lucine had surprised me on our last anniversary with the deed to a plot in the cemetery across the street. ("What could be more romantic?" she asked when she saw my bemusement.)

Greg heard and liked that. Within a few days he and Jackie had bought a plot, which is about a shortstop-to-first-base throw from ours. We'll be neighbors some fine day.*

Put on the coffee. Cue Silly Wizard. Hey, what are you doing?

---

*Greg finished the book—*Circuit Rider Devotions: Reflections from the Lives of Early Methodist Preachers in North America, Volume 3* (Emeth Press, 2023)—and then started another.

8

Jim Owen

A Saver's Grace, 2023

Jim Owen with his favorite typing student, Kathy Hochul, at Dwyer Stadium. Courtesy of Howard Owens.

The cheapest man in Batavia has died—and we are both richer and poorer for it.

I met Jim Owen in the summer of '69—a phrase later borrowed by a Canadian schlockmeister—when I was nine and he was in his mid-twenties.

As supervisor of MacArthur Park, he installed me as shortstop on the park's nine-to-thirteen-year-old baseball team. This was a stupendously bad move, given that I was the youngest player on a jock-heavy team, and shortstop is the most crucial position in the field. It took him a few games to recognize his mistake, but ever after, till his death in early 2023 at age seventy-nine, Jim greeted me as "my second baseman!" (He tended to confuse such minor matters as infield positions.)

Jim taught typing and coached cross country at a school fifty miles distant, but he maintained ties to his hometown, and in retirement returned to live in the house in which he grew up. Over the last twenty years of his life our paths crossed countless times.

Stories of Jim's penny-pinching—the word does not do his preternatural niggardliness justice—are legion. They would be written off as apocrypha, but for the (often incredulous) witnesses.

There was the time Jim, a confirmed bachelor then in middle age, had a date. He took her to a chain restaurant. (I think it was Bob Evans.) Jim let her know that they were going Dutch. Fine, she said. At meal's end the waitress came with the bill. Jim's date threw in half the total; Jim pulled out a buy one, get one free coupon.

There was no second date.

Or there was the time Jim and Wayne, a local radio personality and voice of our Muckdogs minor-league baseball team, took the bus to New York City, 400 miles to our east. Batavia invades Gotham! The two most frugal bachelors in town alighted at the Port Authority and proceeded to paint the town accountant-eyeshade green.

Jim and Wayne wandered over to Times Square. A Superman impersonator accosted them. The ersatz Man of Steel posed with Jim as Wayne snapped a photo. Superman stuck out his palm for the expected gratuity. Jim uncorked his usual line: "My name is crime, and crime don't pay." Superman was not amused.

"Jim, you have to tip him," advised Wayne. Jim wouldn't. So Wayne reached into his pocket and handed Superman his wage: a quarter. And the two Batavians went on their way, leaving a sputtering superhero in their wake.

Those were milestones, but every day and in every way Jim practiced a cheapness that surely has an entry in the *Diagnostic and Statistical Manual of Mental Disorders*. He routinely swiped all the jams and jellies from tables in restaurants, where he never left tips. (Or picked up checks.)

He hoarded the little shampoos and soap bars and razors from the locker room of his country club, which changed its free toiletries policy in response.

In his daily phone calls to my father, Jim would exult over having found a nickel in the supermarket parking lot.

Despite his ostensible retirement, Jim substitute-taught several days a week in our city schools. He'd bring pens and pencils he had picked up gratis at local businesses and charge students a quarter to borrow a writing utensil. He'd return the quarter if they returned the stylus—but he preferred that they did not, for that gave him license to keep the quarter.

The stories go on and on, and they sound like tall tales, exaggerations for comic effect, but they are not.

Jim fully earned his "cheapest man in town" sobriquet.

And yet . . .

Upon Jim's death, dozens of students from his sub-teaching days left messages on internet sites. Some were quite moving. I was particularly struck by this memory of a high school girl.

> Besides finding out there was a snow day, there was nothing else that quite compared to the joy that was felt when you walked into your classroom to find out Mr. James R. Owen was your substitute for the day.
>
> On my first day of ninth grade—which was technically the second day of school but I was too anxious to go the first day—I had a panic attack, managed to get lost during it, and wound up on the back of the auditorium stage. And there I was sitting in a puddle of my tears, panicked and alone, when I heard the unmistakable voice of Mr. Owen as he asked if I would like a Kleenex. And instead of a Kleenex, he handed me a handkerchief he pulled out of his pocket, which only made me cry harder, because my dad always carried one. So there we sat together on the stage, behind the curtain, not talking, as I cried into his hankie. Eventually, I stopped crying.
>
> But we still just sat together. Maybe a half hour later, Mr. Owen told me a phrase that was also in a sympathy card I received two weeks prior when my dad died: "The pain you feel is immeasurable, but so is the love he had for you." He squeezed my hand three times and asked if I was ready to continue my day. He walked me to my English class and told my teacher he needed my help and that's why I had missed all but five minutes of our class.

I had known Jim almost all my life and I didn't know he had that in him.

Jim's classes were free-for-alls—he was no more capable of imposing discipline on unruly teens than he was of handing a $20 bill to a street beggar—but no matter the course he was putatively teaching, he drilled his charges in local history facts. I doubt if any kid has graduated Batavia High over the last two decades without knowing the name of Batavia's founder (Joseph Ellicott), first mayor (Harvey Burkhart), and legendary high school football coach (Danny Van Detta).

He liked to boast of his most famous student, from years ago and miles away: Kathy Hochul, a one-term congresswoman and lieutenant governor of New York who was elevated (or is it demoted?) to the governorship upon the resignation of the disgraced Andrew Cuomo.

In the fortnight interregnum between Cuomo's resignation announcement and Hochul's assumption of office, Jim was present at the opening of a time capsule at his country club. Buried in 1996—not exactly the ancient days of King Arthur or even Chester Alan Arthur—its contents included a photo of several country club members. Among them was Jim, who was wearing the same shirt in the 1996 photo as he was at the capsule's opening. As the boys were ribbing him, Jim's phone rang. He brightened to hear the voice at the other end. "It's Kathy Hochul," he announced to the crowd. Sure, Jim. As if the incoming governor, in the midst of navigating the storm before the calm, would phone . . . *you*.

To quiet the Doubting Thomases, Jim put La Hochul on speakerphone—and sure enough, 'twas her.

The new and largely unknown governor was the subject of quickie biographical stories in the press. Jim happily supplied approbatory quotes to the *New York Daily News* about his old student, praising the superlative typing skills she had demonstrated as a teenager. Folks chided this tightwad Republican for shilling on behalf of a conventional liberal Democrat, but Jim understood that friendship must always trump politics.

In mid-2022, Jim was diagnosed with stage four esophageal cancer. As is surely typical in such cases, he couldn't quite believe it was happening to him. His physical decline was gradual, then precipitous. One week he was tooling around town, attending any public reception offering free food, and the next he was in the hospital, gravely ill. Jim hadn't been abed for more than a week before a hundred or so high school students crammed into the hospital's lobby and serenaded him with Christmas carols. Frail as he was, Jim, eyes clouded and voice whispery, sat in his wheelchair and fist-bumped the kids as they passed by.

By Christmas Day he was in Crossroads House, the local hospice. A doula—a word new to me—said that no resident had ever had so many visitors. Former students poured in as if streaming from a firehose. Jim's room contained an enormous posterboard on which dozens and dozens of high schoolers had written messages of love and mercy and unadorned pleas not to "leave us yet."

One of my visits could have been a scene in some gentle comedy. His naked body curled under a blanket, Jim struggled to speak. "Billy," he rasped, "when it's near the end, you realize something." I leaned my ear closer. What do you realize at the end?

Jim fell asleep. I never did learn this secret. Perhaps it is only vouchsafed to those on the verge.

I last visited Jim a day or two before his death. He was barely conscious, though the folks at Crossroads assured me he could hear. A volunteer told me that "he needs permission to die." I guess she meant that because Jim had no family left and spoke of his religious faith only in the vaguest terms, he needed his friends to urge him on. I didn't say anything quite so straightforward as that, but I did recall to him our old baseball team, reeling off as many names as I could remember. I told him that he was a great Batavia character whom we would never forget. He was able to move his hand slightly, which I took as a sign he was hearing me. Then I whispered to Jim that I'd see him on the other side and I left.

In his final weeks and after his death, the outpouring of community affection for this idiosyncratic character was astounding. A packed house celebrated the naming of the high school auditorium after Jim's father, who in his thirty-seven-year career had founded the school band and chorus. (Octogenarians tell me that the old man was a martinet, but we'll let that pass.) The high school announced "be kind" activities that, because they were tied to the students' memories of this specific, flesh-and-blood and all too human man, packed meaning beyond the usual platitudinous nullities.

My decades-long prediction has been that Jim, whose parents and siblings are dead, and who has no relatives that I know of, would bequeath a small fortune to some community essential—the hospital or museum or suchlike—and half a century from now, when those who have sighed or chuckled over the buy one get one free coupon and crime not paying and a freezer full of stolen jellies have departed this vale of laughter, he will be lauded as the town's great philanthropist.

His estate has been settled. Suffice to say that there will be Owen Rooms and Owen Scholars for many years to come.

Rest in peace, Jim. I promise to put a quarter on your grave every Memorial Day.

SNAPSHOTS

9

Harriet Tubman

In a Child's Eye, 2006

Harriet Tubman in Auburn. Library of Congress/public domain.

Araminta Ross, later known as Harriet Tubman and best remembered as Moses, the preternaturally wise conductor who never lost a passenger on the Underground Railroad, is perhaps the historical personage most familiar to the latest generation of American schoolchildren. The bare facts of her life—escape from slavery, daring raids to rescue other bondsmen from servitude, untimely fits of narcolepsy, service as a Union spy in South Carolina—are extraordinary, but most textbooks are too rigid and unimaginative to convey any sense of what Harriet Tubman was really like.

If only a good novelist had known her, the reader murmurs. Well it just so happens . . .

Tubman made her home in Auburn, New York, on property that had belonged to Lincoln's secretary of State and her ardent admirer, William Seward. And it was in Auburn, a generation removed from the War, that Harriet met a boy named Samuel Hopkins Adams, the fortunate son of a notably cultured Upstate family.

Young Adams had inherited an ample sense of self-worth from his grandsires, who were the subject of Adams's best book, *Grandfather Stories* (1955). As Adams told the tale, a "visiting New England lady" once accosted his paternal grandfather.

> "Adams? Adams? Do you claim kinship with the Boston Adamses?"
>
> "There is a Boston branch, I believe," he answered cautiously.
>
> "I refer to the Presidential Adamses," the lady said haughtily.
>
> "Ah! I was personally acquainted with the Honorable John Quincy Adams. A very respectable gentleman. He may well have been a connection of our line, though, being no brag-hard, he would naturally not press the claim."

The New York Sam Adams, too, would grow into a crusty character. When the forceful old boy was a forceful young boy, his days were not infrequently occupied by visits from "Aunt Harriet" Tubman. Sam's great-aunt, Sarah Hopkins Bradford, had written a pair of books about Tubman, and it was because of Aunt Harriet that young Sam and his friends played slaves and overseers rather than cowboys and Indians.

Harriet Tubman would walk the two miles to Adams's maternal grandfather's house. Grandfather Hopkins would ask, "Harriet Tubman, will you sing for my grandchildren?" and after a modest demurral Harriet "would clap her stringy hands upon her bony knees, rock her powerful frame, snap her eyes," and sing "Go Down, Moses" in the same great baritone in which she once sang her song of deliverance to escapees following the North Star.

The children, being children, would make impertinent requests ("Show us your mark, Aunt Harriet"), and she would reveal the scars left by the whip.

Harriet Beecher Stowe's dramatics left Harriet Tubman unimpressed: "When our grandmother once took her to a matinee of *Uncle Tom's Cabin,*" Adams recalled, "she expressed approval of the theme but was critical of Eliza's escape across the ice, declaring the affair ill-managed and intimating that she could have handled it better."

" 'Bloodhoun's!' she said disdainfully, eyeing the two disconsolate mastiffs who appeared in the role. 'I nevah made no min' of bloodhoun's.' " (Adams transcribed Tubman's remarks in her rich dialect, and while it may strike our ears as awkwardly anachronistic he also captures her in a way that later writers, hamstrung by etiquette and not having had the benefit of her acquaintance, cannot.)

Although her date of birth remains a mystery, Harriet Tubman lived close to if not beyond ninety years. She was a fixture about town, and often was seen sweeping clean the front yard of the Harriet Tubman Home, which her respectful neighbors in Auburn had endowed as a residence for indigent African Americans.

Tubman, one of the great heroines of our history, deserves better than mummification in dry textbooks. We are lucky that Samuel Hopkins Adams, the young novelist-to-be, never forgot her sly wit and superabundant humanity. When Sam and his cousins asked her, "Did you kill lots of people?" Aunt Harriet disappointed them by answering no.

"Why not?" they wondered.

"Whuffoh I want to kill folks?" replied Harriet Tubman. "Nobody nevah kill me."

10

The Brisbanes

The Burgher and the Dreamer, 2022

Albert Brisbane. Courtesy Library of Congress, Prints and Photographs Division. Public domain.

God damn this virus! It's not so much that I mind the coughing—as a schoolboy I heard every mock-hacking variant of "Cough-Man"—as that COVID's wretched timing caused me to miss Opening Day for baseball's Muckdogs for the first time in decades, as well as the premiere of *Brothers at Odds*, a play about our town's eccentric nineteenth-century Brisbane family, whose manse faces an uncertain future.

I did catch the second performance of both play and ballclub, though, and I can report that greed, bigamy, and utopian spider webs are as American as balks and catcher's interference.

Albert and George Brisbane, the titular siblings, were less Cain and Abel than Vain and Stable. My sympathies were with George, a solid burgher who tossed coins to children on his daily walk to the barber shop and in winter carried a magnifying glass, which he used to examine snowflakes that landed on his black coat sleeve.

George's fame extended no further than the verge of Main Street. Albert, by contrast, was America's best-known antebellum proselytizer for a bizarre variant of socialism.

As a boy, Albert stood on the rude bridge arching the Tonawanda Creek and tossed pebbles into the shallow water, asking himself the question no twelve-year-old ponders: "What is the work for man on earth?" When his land-speculating father told Albert that his future was bright, the lad replied, "The great thing, it seems to me, is to know what the human race has to do, and then to cooperate with it in its work."

Rolling his eyes, Pop shipped his annoying son off to boarding school, then sent him on a Grand Tour of Europe that lasted six years. The pilgrim studied with Hegel, bedded strumpets galore, and fell hard for the ideas of the French woolgatherer Charles Fourier, the daft draftsman who proposed that society reorganize into 1,620-person "phalanxes" in which the passions—for work, leisure, and polyamorous rutting—would be indulged for the general benefit. Fourier predicted that his scheme eventually would produce a world in which, writes historian Chris Jennings, "mosquitoes will go extinct; friendly whales will tow our ships, and the oceans . . . will taste like lemonade."

Albert Brisbane was Fourier's most ardent (and wealthiest) apostle, though he renamed the panacea "Associationism" and downplayed his guru's more outre sexual insights, such as that each phalanx would contain an equal number of sadists and masochists. From his perch as a columnist for Horace Greeley's *New York Tribune*, Albert's vigorous evangelism resulted in the creation of forty short-lived phalanxes, most notably Brook Farm, which Nathaniel Hawthorne satirized in *The Blithedale Romance*.

A typical rich socialist, Albert Brisbane somehow avoided sharing the wealth with his neighbors, for example, the poor and pope-ridden likes of my Irish immigrant ancestors. Walt Whitman wrote of our boy: "Somehow or other he always looks as if he were attempting to think out some problem a little too hard for him."

A champion swordsman and deadbeat dad, Albert fathered at least ten children with several women. The last of his wives, Redelia, was a groupie thirty-five years his junior whose friends warned her off the old lech, but what did they know about love?

His young bride later confessed that despite Albert's lofty soul, "in the practical, every-day affairs of life Mr. Brisbane had a multitude of shortcomings." His chronic indigestion was no turn-on for his young newlywed bride, though Redelia offered the tantalizing hint that despite Albert's "vital infirmities, his capacity for endurance seemed immeasurable." I imagine a sigh accompanied that observation, but when you marry a Batavia man, that's what you sign up for.

The play, based on city historian Larry Barnes's entertaining history of the Brisbane family, was written by and starred Genesee Community College professor Derek Maxfield. It is an all-too-rare example of the regional dramaturgy proposed in the 1930s by Wisconsin's Robert Gard, the "Johnny Appleseed of American grassroots theater." To hell with Broadway imperialism. Peoria and Portsmouth don't need local productions of such schmaltz as *Rent* or *Annie*; they need *Brothers at Odds*–style indigenous theater by and for locals.

The exact location of Fourierist Albert Brisbane's cremains is not certain, but stolid brother George's body is six feet under the ground in the old Batavia Cemetery. I left a penny on his gravestone the other day. I prefer snowflake-gazers who flip quarters to kids to world-saving horndogs with dystopian dreams.

11

Mark Twain

Morose and Irritable in the Queen City, 2022

Mark Twain in Buffalo. Artwork by Susan M. Giorgio, from the collection of Bill Kauffman.

"Irreverence is the champion of liberty and its only sure defense," wrote Mark Twain in an age before irreverence became a hanging, or at least exiling, offense.

Perhaps the more meet aphorism today belongs to Edward Abbey: "The distrust of wit is the beginning of tyranny." (The distrust of half-wit, I suppose, is the beginning of a TV critic.)

Mark Twain would be hopelessly out of favor with both wings of the modern duopoly. Militaristic Republicans would scorn Twain for his skepticism of empire and mockery of world-saving cant. (He was a supporter of the Anti-Imperialist League and proposed that the stars and stripes be replaced by the skull and crossbones.) Welfare-state Democrats would choke on such bilious Twainisms as "a maxim of mine is that whenever a man preferred being fed by any other man to starving in independence he ought to be shot."

Happily, Upstate New York registers as among the most politically tolerant sections of the country, so Twain and his works remain an uncanceled presence up here in God's country. The Twain industry is centered in his boyhood home of Hannibal, Missouri, of course, but Upstate cities Elmira and Buffalo played significant roles in the life of the writer christened Samuel Clemens.

Folks leave cigars, not spittle, on Mark Twain's grave in Elmira, hometown of his devoted wife Livy, not to mention the news-reading fabulist Brian Williams and designer of gangbanger garb Tommy Hilfiger. Twain wrote his tales of Tom Sawyer and Huck Finn in Elmira—his octagonal writing hut is open for inspection on the attractive campus of Elmira College—but my subject is Buffalo, whose downtown public library boasts a Mark Twain Room whose star attraction is the original handwritten manuscript of *The Adventures of Huckleberry Finn.*

Twain/Clemens called the Queen City home from August 1869 till March 1871, because Jervis Langdon, his coal monopolist future father-in-law, set him up as part-owner and coeditor of the *Buffalo Express.*

Twain biographers typically dismiss these eighteen months as gelid and miserable, though they were nothing if not eventful. The author married Livy Langdon; was gifted a Second Empire–style mansion on Delaware Avenue, Buffalo's "Millionaires Row," by Livy's father; enjoyed bestseller-dom with *Innocents Abroad*; and roughed out the book that became *Roughing It.*

Buffalo was the place where Mark Twain "decided to stop writing for newspapers and start writing books," says Tom Reigstad in his meticulously researched and richly informative *Scribblin' for a Livin': Mark Twain's Pivotal Period in Buffalo.*

Fitfully active and not quite hail-fellow-well-met—a young city editor recalled his boss as "quiet, reserved, and irritable"—Twain spun out a column for the *Express* consisting of one-liners, odd facts, and facetia. For example,

> "Brigham Young's mother-in-law is dead."
>
> "Mrs. Lucy Morehead Porter, of Covington, has been appointed Postmistress of Louisville, Ky."
>
> "The river Nile is lower than it has been for 150 years. This news will be chiefly interesting to parties who remember the former occasion."

He was no slave to veracity, as evidenced by his account of "John Wagner, the oldest man in Buffalo—105 years," who "recently walked a mile and a half in two weeks. . . . He is to be married next week to a girl 102 years old, who still takes in washing. They have been engaged 89 years, but their parents persistently refused their consent until three days ago." Wagner, Twain averred, "has never tasted a drop of liquor in his life, unless you count whiskey."

At election time he twitted his coeditor in words that could be applied with equal justice to pretty much any political pontificator of our time. His thumb-sucking colleague, said Twain, will "tell you about these candidates as serenely as if he had been acquainted with them a hundred years although, speaking confidentially, I doubt if he ever heard of any of them till to-day."

Twain's departure is often attributed to Buffalo's snow-spangled winters, but the truth is less flaky. He later wrote a friend: "Our year and a half in Buffalo had so saturated us with horrors and distress that we became restless and wanted to change, either to a place with pleasanter associations or with none at all."

During the couple's brief stay in the western edge of New York State, father-in-law Jervis died painfully of stomach cancer; a close school friend of Livy's, visiting from South Carolina, was taken ill with typhoid fever and died in their Delaware Avenue home; and their doomed first child Langdon was born sickly and struggling. (The tot would die shortly after the young family relocated from Buffalo to Hartford, Connecticut.)

Sickness and sadness and death drove the Clemens family out of paradise. I look at the early snow drifting against a backdrop of bare boughs and slate sky and think of Livy and her choleric husband.

12

Josephine Young Case

After Midnight, 2020

Josephine Young Case, youthful poet of hopeful autarky. Wikimedia Commons.

I'll give the coronavirus this: It got me out of going to Buffalo to see the touring company of *Hello, Dolly*.

Well, dark days call for silver linings, don't they?

So when Governor Andrew Cuomo, obviously relishing the near-dictatorial powers he had assumed with nary a peep of protest, ordered the closing of bars, restaurants, theaters, and gyms, and proscribed gatherings of greater than fifty people—or was it ten? I have trouble keeping up with the edicts—I revisited one of the stranger literary artifacts of our haunted region: the book-length blank-verse poem *At Midnight on the 31st of March* by Josephine Young Case.

Published in 1938, during what eventually might be called the First Great Depression, the book is about a little Upstate New York village, Saugersville, which at the stroke of midnight on the last day of March is suddenly, mysteriously, and seemingly irrevocably cut off from the rest of the world. Its two dozen homes, two churches, school, garage, mill, general store, and grange go dark. (Josephine's father, Owen Young, was president of General Electric, and she takes great delight in turning out the lights in what I assume was a winking nod dadward.)

Electric power is gone. The phones are dead. The roads leading out of town have disappeared. Search parties venturing beyond the settlement find only "the endless woods, the silent hills . . . and nowhere any house or any sign of man, there now or ever."

There is "only Saugersville in all the world." It's an autarkist's dream.

Recovering from the initial shock, the good folk of Saugersville take stock. They adapt. They relearn the old ways. Dairymen milk the cows by kerosene light instead of Alec-Tricity. Horses replace farm machinery. Thirsty for beer, they grow hops. Even scoffers head to church.

All is not sunshine and homey bliss. By the following winter influenza cuts through the village; lacking doctors and access to modern medicine, three residents die before "the plague diminished."

There is a *Spoon River Anthology* quality to the poem, with its sensitively incised portraits of Saugersvillians reacting to their village's isolation. Some find satisfaction in communal self-sufficiency, a few rue being stranded in hicksville, and the common lot just make do.

It's look homeward or die, physically and spiritually. "Here is all," resolves the resourceful young May Warder. There is no other place, no better place. I am reminded of a scene in Michael Cimino's *The Deer Hunter*, in which steelworkers Nick (Christopher Walken) and Mike (Robert DeNiro) drunkenly exchange confidences after their friend's wedding on the weekend before they are to be shipped to Vietnam. Mike asks Nick if he thinks they will ever return. Nick says, "You know something? The whole thing. It's right here. I love this fucking place."

Perhaps I ought not advert to a Hollywood movie, even one as good as *The Deer Hunter*, in discussing Case's book, for among the blessings of the little village's severance from the outside is that mass-manufactured culture is no longer imported. Something is lost yet something is gained. A character recalls, "When Saugersville set fashions for itself / I mean to say we had our own ways here / That weren't the ways of Centerfield or Steck / Much less the ways of any city place / Where most of us had never been at all."

Rum and coke and Clark Gable no longer exist, yet the community consensus is that "life is harder than it used to be / But troubles are more real. . . . We're all of us more real, and more alive / And Saugersville is real, more like a town / And not a gas-pump on a concrete road."

Admittedly, our situation today is disanalogous to that in Case's poem. Televised agitprop from Team Blue and Team Red still pollutes our homes. But the response of ordinary folk to crisis is similar.

Although decades of post–nuclear war and zombie movies have conditioned us to expect all hell to break loose unless we are firmly guided by stern rulers, men and women in stressful times usually exhibit cooperative, even neighborly behavior.

The toilet paper hoarders and elbow-throwing shoppers so beloved by TV reporters are atypical. "Despite Hollywood's clichés to the contrary," writes *Reason*'s excellent Jesse Walker, "it is very rare for people to panic during an emergency. And the typical natural or technological disaster is followed not by a *Mad Max* war of all against all but by mutual aid in the rubble. Crime declines. Bottom-up cooperation flowers. Looting is rare, and when it does occur it usually amounts to scavenging, not theft."

In Saugersville, eleven months into the isolation, a young man of learning and ambition who chafes under the new dispensation has an epiphany as he skis the sloping fields outside the village: "I am alive and this is where I live."

The realization fills him with joy and gratitude. May we in these strange days experience our own revelations.

13

Samuel Hopkins Adams

The Muckraker, 1999

Samuel Hopkins Adams, in his usual pose. Public domain/Wikimedia Commons.

Samuel Hopkins Adams—muckraker, Hamiltonian, chronic novelist, curmudgeonly regionalist—is covered by a "shroud of obscurity," according to his biographer Samuel V. Kennedy III. This neglect has deepened over the years despite (or perhaps because of) Adams's Stakhanovite output: The late sage of Owasco Lake makes his sister Upstater Joyce Carol Oates look as though she suffers from a protracted case of writer's block. Over the better part of a century, Adams published more than fifty novels and numberless magazine articles adding up to more than 10 million words. The contours of his career suggest that he was a particularly diligent hack—Kennedy commends his "readable prose," which is not quite extravagant praise—but Mr. Adams's regional works are of lasting value, and he lived with gusto and an admirable Auburn flair.

Samuel Hopkins Adams was born in Dunkirk in 1871, to a liberal Congregationalist minister and his evocatively named wife Hester, descendant of the Declaration-signing Stephen Hopkins. From his father Adams may have inherited a penchant for the easy cause favored by all Right-Thinking People: Sam Adams would spend a distressingly large portion of his career shooting at such barrel-filling fish as quack-medicine peddlers, fraudulent advertisers, and the Harding administration. But his grandfathers Adams and Hopkins fired the boy's imagination. The former, a Rochesterian, told tales of the Erie Canal, on which he once worked and in which Sam (nicknamed "Huck") and his cousins swam.

Grandfather Hopkins, of Auburn, though lacking the cachet of the canaller, introduced Sam and the cousinage to his friend Harriet Tubman, who sang "Go Down Moses" to the young fry and attended a matinee of *Uncle Tom's Cabin* with Sam's grandmother. Adams's recollection of Tubman, "A Slave in the Family," was later collected in *Grandfather Stories* (1955). As Kennedy reveals, in 1945 *Reader's Digest* rejected this little gem for the department that ought to have been known as the "Most Unforgettable White Character I Have Met."

Adams attended Hamilton, where he raised hell and played on the college's first football team. ("Well do I remember Sam Adams," said *New York World* sports editor George Daley, a former Union halfback. "When he made a tackle, bones rattled and the arnica bottle was needed.") Upon graduation he left for the *New York Sun*, a Hamilton haven, and within a decade he was raking muck for *McClure's* and *Collier's*, taking on the beef trust, tuberculosis (which lacked for eloquent defenders), and, as a good Democrat, President Theodore Roosevelt, who snarled of Adams, "I do not regard him as a truthful man."

In 1905, Adams made his mark on American journalism with a six-part series in *Collier's* titled "The Great American Fraud." His exposure of the patent medicine industry, with its absurd claims for inedible syrups and alcohol-soaked panaceas, spurred the passage of the Pure Food and Drug Act.

The duality that runs throughout Upstate political history—earnest reformism on the one hand, and demotic plainspokenness on the other—was embodied in Mr. Adams. He participated in the most ridiculous excesses of World War One propaganda, signing up as a "Four Minute Man" for George Creel's Committee on Public Information and slandering any pacifist, German-American, or socialist who had the temerity to question Mr. Wilson's war—and then in 1940 he joined the America First Committee, convinced that another world war would mean an end to American liberties. He supported prohibition—but once demon rum had been banished from freedom's land by constitutional amendment, he became a latitudinarian who told the *Cleveland Press* that his favorite hobby was "[w]atching my friends violate the Volstead Act."

Adams began writing fiction, confident that "there are only two basic plots: that for the adventure story of which mystery is an offshoot, and that for the love story." His torrential output earned middling reviews and occasionally brisk sales; under the pen name Warner Fabian he wrote the *succes de scandale Flaming Youth* (1923). At least twenty movies, silents and talkies, were made from Mr. Adams's stories and novels, and if most were dogs, Frank Capra did turn "Night Bus" into the smash *It Happened One Night*. (Star Claudette Colbert wrote to a friend after the shooting wrapped up, "I've just finished the worst picture in the world!")

After the Second World War, Mr. Adams turned largely to regional and juvenile fiction; *Canal Town* (1944), his enjoyable novel of Palmyra in the 1820s, can be found on most any Upstate used bookstore shelf. He collected the stories of his forbears, particularly Grandfather Adams, into the charming *Grandfather Stories*, which may well be his most enduring work, and the book that will keep Adams in our hearts and minds for many years to come.

Adams and his second wife, the peppery Jane, who called her beloved "the little bastard" and "the old prune," made Wide Waters, their home beside Owasco Lake, the literary and martini-consuming capital of Central New York. Mr. Adams's ashes were spread over the lake upon his death in 1959, and though he has been forgotten by our often-amnesiac region, he is fortunate that Samuel V. Kennedy III, a neighbor boy from across the lake who attended Adams's memorial service forty-plus years ago, has produced a solid biography of our prolific native son.

Kennedy's subtitle is no mere afterthought: His book contains more details of Mr. Adams's advances, sales, royalties, and the usual writerly requests for loans than most nonaccountant readers will care to know. But Kennedy has done well by Adams; he has atoned for ignoring the old man's advice to choose Hamilton over Cornell those many years ago. Let us hope that Kennedy's is the first leaf in a great flowering of Upstate biography, for we have so many twentieth-century cultural and political figures (Henry W. Clune, Josephine Young Case, Carl Carmer, Barber B. Conable Jr., Kenneth Keating, John Gardner) whose life stories have yet to be told. May Mr. Kennedy's book lead the way.

Vernon Parrington wrote of William Cullen Bryant, "He may not have been a great poet, but he was a great American." Whatever the verdict on the literary worth of Samuel Hopkins Adams, he was a great Upstater.*

---

*A review of Samuel V. Kennedy III, *Samuel Hopkins Adams and the Business of Writing* (Syracuse University Press, 2000).

14

Edward Crone Jr.

Billy Pilgrim Turns Fifty, 2019

Gretel Kauffman at the grave of Edward Crone Jr., Mt. Hope Cemetery, Rochester. Collection of Bill Kauffman.

Edward "Joe" Crone Jr. was a gawky Dumbo-eared boy from the Rochester, New York, suburb of Brighton. Nicknamed "Goony" by the urchin wits of the Twelve Corners neighborhood, he was seemingly born to misplay right field. The highlight of his high school years was his participation in the Stamp Club.

In 1943, Crone was studying engineering at Hobart College but envisioning a life in the ministry when his spindly form was sucked into the vortical hell of the Second World War, wherein he played the part of a private in the 106th Infantry Division.

Hopeless at the martial arts—a fellow soldier recalled that gear was always spilling from his unsecured pack—Joe Crone was taken prisoner by the Germans in the aftermath of the Battle of the Bulge. He survived the Allied bombing of Dresden, which killed upward of 25,000 civilians, thanks to his billeting in an underground meat locker. Yet having lived through one of the most horrific death-dealings of the Second World War, Crone died just weeks later of starvation and what a fellow Dresden prisoner called his "thousand-mile stare."

The crony-less Crone never did become a wealthy optometrist or befriend an obscure science-fiction writer named Kilgore Trout or copulate with a movie star named Montana Wildhack in a human zoo on the planet Tralfamadore. But his fictive doppelgänger, US Army chaplain's assistant Billy Pilgrim, did all that and more in Kurt Vonnegut's antiwar and pro-time travel novel *Slaughterhouse-Five*, that welcome staple of high school English courses whose golden anniversary is upon us.

Naturally, Vonnegut, the "Christ-worshiping agnostic," scion of the First Family of Indianapolis architecture, and slaughterhouse-mate of goofy Joe Crone, would produce a funhouse-mirror pacifist take on what those who never saw action call "the Good War." As a student columnist for the *Cornell Daily Sun*, Vonnegut had vigorously defended antiwar figures of the day, including the most controversial:

"Charles A. Lindbergh is one helluva swell egg, and we're willing to fight for him in our own quaint way. . . . The mud-slingers are good. They'd have to be to get people hating a loyal and sincere patriot. On second thought, Lindbergh is no patriot—to hell with the word, it lost it's [*sic*] meaning after the Revolutionary War. . . . The United States is a democracy, that's what they say we'll be fighting for. What a prize monument to that ideal is a cry to smother Lindy."

Kurt Vonnegut was unsmotherable. Not so poor Joe Crone. A neighbor later recalled him as "a skinny, lanky kid . . . probably the last person

I could ever visualize as an infantry soldier. Holy crow!" Crone traded his skimpy rations to his fellow Dresden POWs for little pieces of candy. "He was just so good-hearted," recalled one ex-POW, that "everybody was beating him out of his food."

"Joe was deeply religious and kind of childlike," said Vonnegut. "The war was utterly incomprehensible to him, as it should have been."

Billy Pilgrim is an inept soldier, hapless and self-abnegating, mocked and derided by his comrades. So Vonnegut waited until Crone's parents had deceased before he revealed to Rochester newsman John Reinan the identity of Billy Pilgrim's model. (Crone's mother, according to friends, "just went bananas" upon receiving news of her only child's death. She "never recovered.")

Arriving in the Flour City in 1995 to deliver a lecture, Vonnegut, who had watched as Crone was buried in Dresden in cerecloths of white paper, was stunned to learn that his buddy Joe had come home. Crone's parents had traveled to Germany in 1950, to disinter his body and rebury it in Rochester's Mt. Hope Cemetery, whose "196 forested acres make one of the loveliest urban walks in New York State," as Steve Huff writes in his necropolitan delight *In Our Home Ground*, a website guide to the graves of the literary in Upstate New York.

The penny I placed on Crone's modest and weathered stele in early May was its first token of the season. (Leaving an FDR-head dime would have been cruel.) His parents rest at his side, and in the company of Susan B. Anthony, Frederick Douglass, Frank Gannett, cinquain poet Adelaide Crapsey, and a cast of many thousands.

Almost a quarter-century ago, and fifty years after the firestorm of Dresden, Kurt Vonnegut stood alone before Joe Crone's grave. His hosts watched him from a respectful distance. Vonnegut smoked a cigarette, talked to the headstone, wept, and finally took his leave. He said softly as he left the cemetery, "Well, that closes the book on World War Two for me."

And so it goes and so it goes and so it goes and so it goes. But where it's going, no one knows.

15

Martha Treichler

Black Mountaineer, 2020

Legend-shrouded Black Mountain College was the experimental school outside Asheville, North Carolina, which for almost a quarter century (1933–1956) incubated, nurtured, and disgorged an era's worth of the holy fools and ragged prophets and pretentious frauds of the postwar American avant-garde and the (in some cases reactionary) counterculture: John Cage, Paul Goodman, Merce Cunningham, Willem de Kooning, and Buckminster Fuller, to name a few.

Yet for my money, the most remarkable couple to pass through Black Mountain was Bill and Martha (Rittenhouse) Treichler, two farm kids, the former an Iowan, the latter a daughter of Maryland, who met and fell in love at Black Mountain during the 1948 to 1949 school year.

You wanna talk Americana? Bill's mother had attended fifth grade with the "American Gothic" painter Grant Wood. Martha was a 4-H all-star who designed and sewed her own clothes. For the six decades after they left Black Mountain, until Bill's death in 2008, they built their own homes from salvaged bricks and native lumber, grew their own food, milled their own flour, raised their own livestock, and brought up five children, whom they read to sleep at night from the works of Walter Scott and Trollope. They also published *The Crooked Lake Review*, a fine journal of Upstate New York culture.

Mildred Loomis, "grandmother of the counterculture," praised the Treichlers as the compleat homesteading family in her volume *Alternative Americas*. They even gave me one of the few satisfying voting-booth experiences of my life, when in 2006 I cast a ballot for the Treichlers' daughter

Rachel when she ran as the Green Party's candidate for New York State Attorney General.

The anarchist spirit of Black Mountain was accompanied by a certain untidiness: Bill Treichler, upon arriving, was "dismayed by the unkempt campus overgrown with high grass and weeds," recalls Martha. When Bill complained to his parents, they sensibly suggested "that he stay and cut the grass." He did. (John Cage sure wasn't going to do it. Nor was "Bob" Rauschenberg, though he did lend Martha his sewing machine.)

The place left a deep mark on the Treichlers, who combined poetical imaginations with hoe-and-axe practicality to a Wendell Berryian degree. It also gave Martha a mentor and even collaborator: the whale-like six-foot, eight-inch poet Charles Olson, best known for harpooning Herman Melville.

The one sour note in Martha's reminiscences—which we shall sweeten—concerns Edward Dahlberg, the novelist and critic who taught briefly at Black Mountain before decamping just weeks into his stay because the city boy found the students "insolent" and the Carolina foliage "homicidal," citing its "savage, serpentine trees and leaves."

Dahlberg had been a member of the Communist Party USA, so he was no stranger to mendacity, and one fib he told of his miserable sojourn at Black Mountain slighted Martha. Happily, it's not too late to set the record straight.

In Martin Duberman's history *Black Mountain: An Exploration in Community* (1972), we read: "A girl named Martha Rittenhouse said she'd read Proust over the summer. 'What Proust?' Dahlberg demanded. 'All of it,' Martha answered. 'Why?' Dahlberg asked. 'Because it was there,' said mountain-minded Martha."

Not true, says Martha today, who explains, "I did not say what Dahlberg attributed to me. I had read some of Proust in a French literature course at my previous college, Bridgewater College, and thought him interesting. I was working as a live-in baby sitter and nanny for some rich folks, to save money for college, and after my charges were in bed, I had hours to fill. I read Proust. At Black Mountain I felt Dahlberg was making fun of me for reading the seven novels of Proust in nine months. I resented this."

Duberman continues: "Dahlberg later got even with her; when she gave a disapproving oral report on *Madame Bovary*, regretting in passing that Emma had married 'for reasons of carnal lust,' Dahlberg, ignoring the garbled literary interpretation, shot back at her, 'My dear Miss Rittenhouse, for what reasons *do* you intend to marry?' "

Another lie. Says Martha: "As we discussed the book in class, I commented that I did not think Flaubert treated his character, Dr. Bovary, fairly.

He gives him a club foot, and, I thought at the time, was unjustifiably demeaning to this character. I did not complain that Emma married 'for reasons of carnal lust' and I do not remember Dahlberg's saying, 'My dear Miss Rittenhouse, for what reasons do you intend to marry?' In my opinion, Dahlberg did not treat his students with respect, and as I remember it, I was not the only one who felt this way."

Okay, record corrected.

Martha, who turned ninety-one in February, is still writing; giving readings; canning tomatoes, corn, green beans, and cabbage; and making cider (100 gallons this past fall). In 2020, the Beat-flavored FootHills Publishing will bring out her seventh volume of poetry in the last decade, this one called *Hanging on a Limb*, whose title piece goes:

Year by year
the limb sags a little;
year by year
my hands slip a little;
year by year
my arms tire;
but the view is spectacular.*

*Martha died in November 2023. In 2020 she was feted as a major and underknown contemporary American poet by Howard Nelson in *The Hollins Critic*.

16

Jackson C. Frank

Radio Free America, 2018

Bill Kauffman at the grave of Jackson C. Frank. Photo by Mark Dee.

When the mellowly wry Richard Beatty asked me to help him spin platters—well, touch buttons—as a guest-host on his streaming *Geezer Radio* show, I accepted the invite, after making it clear that I was a relative stripling and in no sense a codger, dotard, or anywhere near geezerdom.

Our theme was "Forgotten Songs of the 1960s," so my thoughts turned immediately to two obscure singer-songwriters once hailed by hopeful blurb-writers as "the next Bob Dylan."

Eleven-year-old Jackson C. Frank made *Life* magazine in 1954 for an incident that nearly took his life. The sixth-grader survived a boiler-room explosion in his suburban Buffalo elementary school that killed fifteen of his classmates and left him painfully, perpetually scarred. (He did get to meet well-wishers Elvis and Kirk Douglas.)

Upon hitting twenty-one, Frank collected $80,000 from the insurance company and sailed to England, where he blew it all on Aston Martins, Bentleys, wine, and women. With a poetically elegiac streak and an unusual guitar technique necessitated by his gnarled fingers, Frank burst supernova-like on England's developing folk music scene. Paul Simon, then resident in London, produced Frank's self-titled (and only) album, which featured an achingly morose masterpiece called "Blues Run the Game."

The album tanked commercially. Frank repatriated. He ate. And drank. His mind wandered till it had shaken loose of any mooring. Within a shockingly brief time, the Buffalo boy with the shy disarming smile and talent for turning a melancholy lyric had become an obese homeless paranoid-schizophrenic. The days of wine and roses, not to mention dating models, were gone. The blues had run, and then won, the game.

At one point, the corpulent and crapulent Frank begged Paul Simon for a handout. According to Frank's biographer Jim Abbott, Simon, no comrade in alms, gave him $1,500 in exchange for a promissory note and the rights to Frank's music.

"Hello darkness, my old friend" indeed.

Frank's hardships mounted. He had an eye shot out by a juvenile delinquent with a pellet gun. He was in and out of asylums. He grew fatter and stranger and then in 1999 he died, leaving as his legacy that one lovely album.

But there are stirrings of rebirth. "Blues Run the Game" is covered with encouraging frequency. Fellow Buffalonian Vincent Gallo, the Calvin Klein model/auteur/Republican, used Frank's "Milk and Honey" in the soundtrack to *The Brown Bunny* (2003), his cult road picture with a Triple XXX climax. Buffalo boys gotta stick together.

No posthumous renaissance seems to be in the cards for my other Dylan manque, the late Carl Oglesby, the New Left visionary with a sympathetic understanding of Middle America.

Carl was a working-class kid from Ohio, a playwright who stepped away from a budding career in the military-industrial complex to serve as president of Students for a Democratic Society in 1965 to 1966. In his seminal 1967 essay "Vietnamese Crucible," he linked the "American libertarian right" with "the Negro freedom movement and the student movement against Great Society–Free World imperialism," concluding that "the Old Right and the New Left are morally and politically coordinate."

Oglesby's SDS, built on "freewheeling participatory democracy," collapsed in the bombast and bomb-blast of the Weather Underground. In his memoir, *Ravens in the Storm* (2008), Carl wrote of his final break with the mirthless ideologues who destroyed SDS.

Talk about two paths diverging! Carl—swimming in the native radical stream, aware of the possibilities that underlie prosaic surfaces—had proposed opening channels to Rotarians, Elks, the PTA, and church groups. Privileged Weatherbrats like his erstwhile friend Bernardine Dohrn, the "Dig it!" cheerleader for the Manson Family, scoffed. "Where are you coming from?" Dohrn asked in horror. Oglesby replied, with a world of meaning, "Ann Arbor, Kent, Akron, Kalamazoo."

Carl was expelled from SDS. The harridan who conducted his show trial accused him of being "trapped in our early, bourgeois stage" and lacking "a Marxist-Leninist perspective."

What's a red-blooded American boy to do? Pick up a baseball, a gun, a hoe, a wrench, a pen, or a guitar. Carl chose the guitar. On the advice of *Village Voice* writer Nat Hentoff, Maynard Solomon of Vanguard Records signed him. He released two albums of Beat-spirited, country-inflected folk music. *Carl Oglesby* (1969) and *Going to Damascus* (1971) are full of wry observations, Dylanesque wordplay, goofy titles ("Play Volleyball Just Like a Man"), and songs dedicated to, among others, Gene Kelly, Leslie Caron, and the Weather Underground.

The albums sank like stones half a century ago, but today they sound more like sunken treasures. Check 'em out.

Late in life, Carl saw the rerelease of his albums on CD, though when I asked him if this presaged an Oglesby revival, he laughed the laugh of the resigned, saying, "Don't hold your breath."

I'm not. Blues run the game. But now and then a guy catches a break.

17

Midge Costanza

The Democracy, 1974

Midge Costanza, populist Democrat. Collection of Bill Kauffman.

Bryan Adams, born within a fortnight of yours truly, waxed profitably wistful over his summer of '69, but I shall extol, for rather less remuneration, the autumn of '74.

The goad is my editing of the newly published *Congressional Journal of Barber B. Conable, Jr., 1968–1984*. I was honored to undertake the task; the late Mr. Conable, with whom I became friends in my adulthood, is without question the greatest public man to hail from our boondock. Selected on different occasions as the most respected member of the House of Representatives, the Republican Conable had among his many charming quirks a refusal to accept campaign contributions greater than $50. He kept to this limit—which his peers regarded as evidence of suicidal puritanism—even in the Democratic landslide year of 1974, when Conable was outspent nearly two-to-one by labor-backed Midge Costanza, the charismatic vice mayor of Rochester, who would parlay her high-profile defeat into an eventful twenty-month spin as assistant for public liaison under Jimmy Carter.

My younger brother and I must have stuck upward of a thousand Costanza for Congress flyers under windshield wipers that fall. When Midge came to town she'd make a big deal over her young go-fers. I've heard she had a temper and the vocabulary of a sailor but she sure was sweet to us.

Midge Costanza was the daughter of a sausage-maker, a girl from an urban front-porch neighborhood whose prepolitical job was in the concrete-mixing business. Her campaign speeches gave cheap demagoguery a bad name, but she delivered them with spunk and style and Italian feist. Midge, with her high school education, would be an outlier today in a party that has been colonized by smug professionals. Midge later decamped to Southern California; uprooted from that which had formed her, she blanched into a standard liberal Democrat. She also inched out of the closet. But she lives in my memory as a fiery populist who shared the concerns of the un-degreed.

One cannot overstate just how different the parties were in those days before antisocial media and vapid thirty-somethings disgorging dreary orthodoxy with comely outrage over the idiot box combined to nationalize political discourse and chase the soak-the-rich, family-first, blue-collar workers out of the Democratic Party and the well-read, liberal-minded middle class out of the Republican Party.

I suppose there were a few eggheads and sob sisters in our small-town Democracy, but I never met them while licking envelopes in the union hall under the benevolent supervision of local labor leader Putzy Pietrovito. Those old, salt of the earth Dems bring to mind Thoreau's line about John

Brown: "He would have left a Greek accent slanting the wrong way, and righted up a falling man."

What a year 1974 was in New York politics. The successful Democratic candidate for governor, Hugh Carey, was a liberal Brooklyn Irish Catholic. Carey was the best, or least bad, governor we've had since Al Smith almost a century ago, but as an intermittently prolife liberal he'd be a pariah in today's party. (No less than that arbiter of morality Andrew Cuomo has said that right-to-lifers "have no place in the state of New York.")

For his part, Barber Conable was a prochoice federalist who wished to leave abortion law to the states. He respected Carey but suspicioned that the Pope occupied too large a place in the Irishman's political calculations.

For US Senate, Democrats nominated Ramsey Clark, perhaps the most left-wing major party candidate ever to run for statewide office. Clark, who had served as attorney general to the uncivilly unlibertarian LBJ before his sinistral stretch, would make the callow wokesters of the AOC camp look like Joe Manchin.

If ever Ramsey Clark could be elected senator it would have been in 1974, when Republicans were reeling from Watergate, and incumbent GOP Senator Jacob Javits, an able but arrogant man who was never popular in Upstate New York, lost the "you've-got-no-one-else-to-vote-for" Republicans to Conservative Party nominee Barbara Keating, the attractive widow of a US Marine killed in Vietnam.

It's hard to believe, but New York was a competitive state back then. Carey trounced incumbent Republican Malcolm Wilson (whom Conable called "an empty oil can"), but Javits and Keating combined for over 60 percent of the vote against Clark.

Today's pathetic New York State Republican Party barely bothers to run candidates for state comptroller and attorney general and throws in the towel against the unprepossessing senatorial duo of Wall Street errand-boy Chuck Schumer and the frivolous Kirsten Gillibrand.

It's a long way from 1974. I no longer have a Minnesota Vikings poster on my bedroom wall, and peppery working-class champions like Midge Costanza and liberal micks who accept Church teachings like Hugh Carey are as absent from the New York Democratic Party as rectitudinous rural intellectuals like Barber Conable are from the Republican Party.

18

Danny

Vanishing Point, 2019

My friend Danny fell harder, faster, and farther than any man I have ever known.

When he wasn't following the Grateful Dead, Danny was an attorney representing black lung–diseased coal miners in Western Pennsylvania. His father had been a vocal partisan of George Wallace (for whom a lot of those miners probably voted) but the son swung from the left side of the plate. The only politician I ever heard him extol was the Kentucky drug-legalization gadfly Gatewood Galbraith, who billed himself as the "last free man in America." I think Danny's ambition was to be what Cleavon Little hailed in the cult film *Vanishing Point* (1971) as "the last beautiful free soul on this planet."

He didn't quite make it.

As boys, our families spent every New Year's Eve together. We kids would take one bite of a piece of candy seconds before midnight, and then finish it after the clock struck 12, so that we could say it had taken us two years to eat the thing. A (truncated) lifetime of kindred foolishness followed.

Booze and sports, sports and booze. Those two elements were part of our every infrequent meeting as adults. But I'm afraid the booze became Danny's constant craving.

Reversing the Hemingwayesque "first gradually, and then suddenly" pattern, Danny died suddenly, and then gradually.

In his late forties, and in astonishingly short order, it all collapsed. His wife left him. He had a stroke. He had a heart attack. He was convicted of felony drunk driving. He was sent to prison for a year. (I asked him what the inmates called prison. The joint? The rock? The Big House? "Just prison," said Danny, whose nickname therein was Oldhead.)

He was disbarred. He lost his home. He returned to his natal Upstate New York and lived in an inner-city halfway house, where he was beaten senseless and robbed by two thugs. (I hope they enjoyed the buck-fifty or so they found in his threadbare wallet.)

And then things got *really* bad.

But first, Danny found God, or God found Danny.

He joined an urban church, which provided the peace, serenity, and fellowship that the liquor and the drugs never could. "If you had told me twenty or thirty years ago that I would become a member of a Baptist church I would have said you're crazy," he testified in one of the videos he made for his new refuge. He read the Bible, he edited the church newsletter, he gave legal advice to those in trouble, and he listened to and loved the addicted.

Hitting bottom, he ascended.

But as the luckless protagonist of *Detour*, one of those film noirs Danny so loved, dourly reflects, "Whichever way you turn, fate sticks out a foot to trip you."

Fate blinked; Danny lost his mind. The doctors diagnosed him with Creutzfeldt-Jakob disease, disorderly cousin to mad cow disease. The prognosis was beyond grim: rapid-onset dementia, hallucinations, psychosis, muscular rigidity, death.

In his right mind, Danny would have made a joke of it: "Mad cow disease? Are you fuckin' kidding me?"

He never knew what hit him, thank God. Committed to a hospital for the indigent, he wandered the hallways for many months, well beyond his projected date of death, a solitaire in a milling crowd of the brain-damaged.

"Hi, Bill," he would greet me, and then the lights would dim. He knew that he was a lawyer, and that Roger Staubach and Craig Morton had split quarterbacking duties for the Dallas Cowboys in 1971, but beyond that all was murk and fog. The only thing Danny ever had and never lost was his great stertorous *har-har-har* laugh, which I could educe by recalling some escapade of the distant past. Whether he remembered any of it I've no idea.

His sweet mother, enduring serious medical problems of her own, as well as caring for her rapidly invaliding second husband, visited him regularly. Hers was the saddest love of all.

Danny died earlier this year. The minister at the church of his boyhood, an old high school classmate of his, departed from the Presbyterian *Book of Order* and sang the Grateful Dead's "Ripple."

Reach out your hand if your cup be empty
If your cup is full may it be again
Let it be known there is a fountain
That was not made by the hands of men.

I was never a Deadhead—punks hated those interminable jams and that whole languid hophead hippie trip—but if God is in the roses and the thorns then surely He is in the fountains of youthful indiscretion and Oldhead discernment.

Drink up, Danny. We'll meet again.

19

Steve Huff

Grave Matters, 2023

Gravestone of John Gardner. Photo by Lucine Kauffman.

Prose may be deathless, but authors are not, and some of us honor those who compose with visits to where they decompose. I'm afraid that I am one such pilgrim: heck, my wife left her bridal bouquet at the grave of Jack Kerouac in Edson Cemetery in Lowell, Massachusetts. The epitaph for "Ti Jean," as that soulful Canuck was known, is "He Honored Life"; so, paradoxically, do those who make sepulchral sorties.

The noted poet Steve Huff knows his way around a necropolis, and he brings us along for the ride in his new book, *Resting Among Us: Authors' Gravesites in Upstate New York* (Syracuse University Press). Huff wants "to help raise Upstate New Yorkers' awareness of our literary heritage." Our schools have failed miserably at this task, as state and local history have been squeezed out of a teach-to-the-test system. More's the pity, as pound for pound, Upstate can slug it out with anyone—we can even go fifteen rounds with the champ, Mississippi.

You doubt me? Then I'll bid Washington Irving, James Fenimore Cooper, Mark Twain (he wrote *The Adventures of* both *Tom Sawyer* and *Huckleberry Finn* in Elmira), and Edmund Wilson . . . for openers.

This being Upstate New York, Huff's subjects include Theosophists (Claude Bragdon, Matilda Joslyn Gage) and drunks (Charles "*The Lost Weekend*" Jackson, Frederick Exley) and, to borrow from Cher's classic tale of woe on the road, gypsies (Paul Bowles), tramps (Edna St. Vincent Millay), and thieves (Ned Buntline).

Bowles's ashes ended up in rural Lakemont instead of under his sheltering sky because he passed childhood summers in a nearby family cabin. He was one of us only in death, unlike the dipsomaniacal memoirist Exley, who once said of his hometown that "Watertown is not in my marrow; it *is* my marrow." And now Exley is in *its* earthy marrow. His poignant epitaph is taken from his classic novel of failure, *A Fan's Notes*: "It was my fate, my destiny, my end, to be a fan."

Mention of Exley leads naturally to Robert Lax, the experimental poet who spent most of his adulthood on the island of Patmos. Lax is buried in Olean, from which fastness he perhaps exercises his fandom on behalf of the Bonnies of St. Bonaventure. I can imagine him poetizing, in characteristic Lax style:

MAKE basket
make BASKET
ple-ASE

Fran Striker, creator of *The Lone Ranger*, rests peacefully forty-five minutes south of us in Arcade. Admittedly, we're not trespassing on the *belles lettres* here, but as Huff points out, ole' Franny sure knew how to mint pop-culture nuggets: "Hi-ho, Silver!" "Ke-mo-sah-bee," "Who was that masked man?" and "silver bullet" dripped from his pen.

And while we're talking high art, when next you are in Madison County you might pay homage to Walter R. Brooks, whose articulate animal stories were harvested to create *Mr. Ed*, the talking horse of the 1960s TV series. Steve Huff, admirably eager to defend his fellow Upstaters against Hollywood vulgarization, notes that the idiot box not only moved Ed's locale to Southern California but metamorphosed "the often tipsy Wilbur Pope to a more staid Wilbur Post, and his intemperate horse was made likewise more discreet."

Anyone up for a faithful reboot of *Mr. Ed*?

I've visited a handful of these sites. I have burbled gratitude to the remains of Utica's Harold Frederic, whose work I adapted for the feature film *Copperhead*, and I've stood mutely in Rochester's Holy Sepulchre before Louise Brooks, the bobbed-hair beauty who wrote a wonderfully acerbic book (*Lulu in Hollywood*) about the silent-film era.

Each Memorial Day I leave a penny on the stone of John Gardner, my town's contribution to American fiction. Gardner's modest stone reads, somewhat immodestly, "All he spoke or cast was mysterious and holy."

But there are so many cemeteries, so little time before we check into what the choleric Algonquin Roundtable wit Alexander Woolcott, ensconced in the cemetery of his beloved Hamilton College, called "the last dormitory."

I hope someday to pay my respects to Dorothy Day on Staten Island, Gore Vidal in DC's Rock Creek Cemetery, and Edward Abbey in the Cabeza Prieta Desert in Arizona, but in the meantime I'm giving thanks for Steve Huff's generous spirit. "I do *not* call myself a scholar, nor a historian, only a writer in search of the ancestors of my tribe," he writes, but I call him a resurrectionist, for by visiting gravesites he has brought our forebears back to life.

20

Wanda Frank

The Play's (Not) the (Whole) Thing, 2019

The irrepressible Wanda Frank. Courtesy of WBTA Radio.

"Knowledge and love of a place is a large part of the joy in people's lives. There must be plays that grow from all the countrysides of America, fabricated by the people themselves, born of their happiness and sorrow."

So said Robert Gard, the Kansas-born "Johnny Appleseed of American grassroots theater," whose promising experiments in Wisconsin, North Dakota, Upstate New York, and elsewhere were casualties of the domestic fallout from the Second World War, which produced "frenzied writing on war-time themes," but no more "home-grown plays on country stages."

Ah, but the muses never really die.

The late Wanda Frank was the cultural czarina of 1960s Batavia. From her perch as the hostess of Frankly Speaking on radio station WBTA, she reviewed school plays, interviewed demi-eminences appearing on the Buffalo stage (I recall Anthony Newley), and opined on trends in theater and film (too much profanity!).

Flash forward to 2007. Though Wanda was an octogenarian, she hadn't lost much on her curveball. She'd been quite a looker way back when, and was not unaware of the fact; she still sauntered through life assuming that your answer to any of her questions would be Yes.

Wanda had been the pistol who restarted the Batavia Players in the 1970s—she received a "break a leg" telegram from Thornton Wilder when she directed "Our Town"—and with her blithe spirit she thought that senectitude was the perfect time to hone her playwriting skills. So she had written an autobiographical trilogy taking her from childhood through middle age and into—let's slip into Wanda-speak here—sassy seniordom.

Wanda rang. I picked up the phone. She wanted our daughter to play little Wanda, and just maybe there was another part for a member of the family.

"My mother was a beautiful woman," Wanda told me, "but she was cold and cruel. Lucine would be perfect."

Mirthfully I relayed this conversation to my wife, who gave me the evil eye but took the part.

The show was . . . unlike any other I have seen.

The first one-act of the trilogy, *Peach Basket*, concerned little Wanda's allergy to peaches, and the inexplicable rage this induced in her mother. Wanda, usually a fussy director, insisted that an ostensible basket of peaches, which played a critical role in the story, be filled with apples, even though the play went up in August, when fresh peaches were plentiful.

"They'll never notice" was the assumption, though of course the perplexed whispers of "aren't those apples?" susurrated through the theater.

The trilogy's other oddities—the men at the Ford gumball factory wolf-whistling and tossing handfuls of gumballs at ten-year-old Wanda as she walks by; an unsourced argument between estranged siblings over a Buffalo Bills cap—served, ingeniously, to detach us from the illusion that B follows A and guided us, slip-slidingly sideways, into Wanda's universe. I absolutely loved it.

But this was an arrant throat-clearing, a veritable *Dubliners* before the *Ulysses*, for Wanda's masterpiece, *Grandpa's Home for Christmas*, which aired over WBTA radio in the season of joy.

We possess what I believe to be the only bootleg tape of this production, and every December we gather 'round my circa 1980s tape recorder, pop the cassette in, drizzle eggnog into the glasses, and away we go!

This forty-minute radio drama concerns the widower Grandpa—played with just the right touch of Robert Mitchum–esque "Baby I don't care" sleepiness by the late velvet-voiced DJ Jerry Warner—as he returns from retirement in Arizona to spend the holidays with his son, daughter-in-law, and two grandchildren in Batavia.

The family strolls the snow-covered sidewalks of the old hometown, Grandpa reminiscing about the olden days while the kids, in a radical departure from verismilitude, boast Babbittishly about the "incredible!" properties of the new city hall.

If you've seen even one Hallmark Christmas special, you'll know that Grandpa is being groomed for a move back home.

But then out of the blue, Grandpa chirps, "There's nothing here for me," and, to our astonishment, he declares his intention to fly back to Arizona "on the earliest possible" flight out.

Who saw *that* coming?

Wanda always heeded the inner voice, no matter how perverse.

Her legacy, the revived Batavia Players, now puts on a dozen shows a year, and usually at least one of them is homegrown. This March our venerable friend Norm, the avuncular Nestor of the troupe, will be King Lear in what he says will be his farewell performance. (We still tease Norm about his role in Wanda's trilogy, wherein his key line was the non sequitur "Mother always said I was good in the kitchen.")

Wanda's dramaturgy zigged when we expected it to zag, but she was Robert Gard's dream walking. I prefer apples to peaches anyway, and if that old coot Grandpa wants to fry in Arizona, let him.

21

Coleen Dwyer

Coffee with Coleen, 2021

Coleen Dwyer in a rare still moment. Photo by Lucine Kauffman.

I've eaten a lot of breakfasts in my time—hell, it must be approaching 20,000 by now—and few if any have equaled those consumed at Coleen's Kitchen on Main Street in the lived-in Erie Canal village of Brockport, New York.

It takes a few minutes before you sense that there's something not quite wrong about Coleen's.

Upon entering the restaurant you pour your own coffee at the beverage station. Maitre d' Coleen directs you to your seat. She hands you the extensive four-page menu, which warns that "you will be charged 59 cents if you ask what kind of bread I have." Read it well and don't waste Coleen's time, you lazy bum!

Waitress Coleen takes your order. She repairs to the grill, where chef Coleen whips up your omelette, scramble, or stack of pancakes and then brings it to your table. When you're done eating she will hand you your check. You walk to the register and cashier Coleen takes your money. After you depart Coleen will bus your table and wash your dishes, all while tending to as many as twenty other patrons seated in the six booths and at the counter.

First-timers don't quite believe what they're seeing. It's as if they've gone to a baseball game and the same guy is pitching, catching, batting, and taking tickets.

At every booth Coleen posts "Rules to Eat By." They're not just ha-ha cutesy. To paraphrase Johnny Rotten, she means it, man.

Coleen requests:

1. DEVICES: Please silence all devices. If you must take a call, please step outside—the restroom is not a phone booth.

2. CHILDREN: Please silence loud and misbehaving children. If you are unable to do that, please take them outside.

3. LANGUAGE: Believe it or not, most of us don't use the word F**K in casual conversation in public. Please show some respect for the people around you.

4. VOLUME: You'd think the phrase "please use your inside voice" would only be necessary for small children. Sadly, this is not the case. Once again, please consider the people around you, including myself.

DO YOU SENSE A THEME?

The only rule necessary should be: PLEASE BE CONSIDERATE OF OTHERS. If this is unacceptable to you, there is a lovely diner right down the street. Thank you, Coleen.

P.S. NO WHISTLING!

My wife, who has an auditory system as sensitive as that of Roderick Usher's, loves these rules, and despite my outdoor voice and regrettably frequent recourse to profanity I'm a fan, too.

Cell-phone honkers and *f*-bombardiers compare her to *Seinfeld*'s Soup Nazi, but in Coleen Dwyer, fifty-six, you can still see the spirited girl from Auburn, New York, who at seventeen ran away to New York City.

Over a plate of raspberry-peach pancakes I chat with Coleen. She tells me that she learned to bake at Wegmans, the noted Rochester grocery chain, before she and her husband, who runs Shag's Record Emporium up the street, moved to Brockport in 1997. Four years later she opened Coleen's Café, which she redubbed Coleen's Kitchen because "people would come in and say what kind of café doesn't have espresso or put lemon in your water?"

She hired coeds from Brockport State College as part-timers for a while, but when the economy took a dive in 2008 she decided to make this a one-woman operation.

Coleen turns on the lights in her kitchen at 4 a.m. and ends the workday taking out the trash at 2:30 p.m. She makes whatever she can from scratch: bagels, five kinds of bread, corned beef hash. At 6 a.m. the regulars, mostly retirees and folks on their way to work, start coming by. The college people, who compose perhaps half her clientele, file in midmorning. She approves of the young 'uns: "They're nice and polite and thoughtful. They speak to adults better than generations before," especially Generation X, which she "found to be the most irritating people. The dude generation. Guys could not get out a sentence without uttering the expletive."

Her rules came in with the advent of the ubiquitous cell phone. On rare occasions she ejects a patron, and she is unrepentant. Not for Coleen the servile and cringing "customer is always right" motto.

She concedes that during the 8:30 to 10:30 a.m. rush customer service can suffer. "If somebody has questions I might be a little short with them because I have to go flip that other guy's eggs over. But I will never give up the quality of the food."

Coleen figures she has another fifteen years of solo breakfast artistry in her, as long as her knees hold out. “I’d like to leave the place feeling that I’ve done the best I can for as many years as I can.”

I’m in awe, and if you don’t like it you can just leave, bud.

22

Thomas

Life in a Cage, 2017

Genesee County Jail. Photo by Mike Kauffman.

I got a story, ain't got no moral

Let's call him Thomas. I have known him since I was five. His was the first (and only) African American family on my block, circa 1973. They could have timed their arrival better: One of Thomas's older relatives killed his estranged white girlfriend shortly before or after the move, which may have caused a grumble or two in the neighborhood.

We grew up playing baseball and football at MacArthur Park (where no cakes were ever left out in the rain) every summer morning, noon, and early eve of our boyhoods. In high school Thomas was an all-conference basketball player—long, lithe, with a soft touch—but college was not in his future.

Thomas's father, with whom he was very close, died when Thomas was barely into adulthood, and the son took to drink. Boy, did he take to it. He had some brushes with the law, but they were alcohol-related, never anything violent. He lost his driver's license long ago and for the last decade or two has been a regular on our streets, teetering along on his trusty bike ("my horse"), weaving and bobbing, and through the grace of God avoiding serious accident.

When we would see each other on the street we would stop and chat. I never saw him sober, but he would grow almost eloquent talking about the old days, about Sheehan's towering home runs and Shep's jarring tackles and how Alex always dropped the long bombs. He was content in this place; he had sojourned in Rochester long ago, but disliked the danger and anonymity of the big city. With a shrug of his shoulders he explained, "I'm a small town guy."

Thomas hated to beg. Like Frank Sarsfield in Russell Kirk's ghost story, "Watchers at the Strait Gate," he kept a running ledger of debts in his head—and he'd pay back his almoners a buck or two at a time. But I'd give him a dollar if he was short, and in the pouring rain I might drive him to the liquor store.

You will tell me that I should have lectured him, driven him to rehab, arranged for an intervention. Sure.

In March 2016 the police were called to Thomas's boyhood home, where he lived still with his elderly and ailing mom (who has since died). In the wee hours of the morning, Thomas and one of his brothers were quarreling. The details are murky. The law claimed that Thomas had a knife, though none was ever found at the scene. A police officer entered the home. The officer reported that Thomas approached him with the knife, so he wisely stepped outside. Thomas retreated to his room upstairs. He finally responded to entreaties to surrender, though—according to police—he was not following directions. He was tasered and taken to county jail, his domicile for the next sixteen months. (He couldn't meet bail, and his stay was extended when he accepted and then rejected a plea deal that would have sent him to prison for three and a half years.)

The background noise to all this emanated from Ferguson, Dallas, and Baton Rouge. "You got bad timing," I said when I first visited Thomas in jail. He smiled ruefully.

"I'm not violent," he said. "You know me, Billy. I never did anything violent. I won't plead to that. I got nephews and nieces in law enforcement. I respect them." So he rolled the dice on a trial.

From my previous experience as a grand-jury foreman I told him to urge his legal defender to fill the jury with as much youth, insolence, marginality, and as many tattoos as possible. No old guys, please. And cut the ponytail.

His attorney never called a single witness. The officer's word was all the jury heard. Despite the evidentiary lack of a weapon—reasonable doubt, anyone?—Thomas was found guilty of menacing a police officer. He was sentenced to three years, and with time already served he'll likely do fourteen months in a state prison hellhole.

I know the police officer's wife, a lovely and talented young woman. The district attorney is a straight arrow and a friend who appeared in the play I wrote for the county's bicentennial. Thomas is a lifelong buddy; his mistakes make no difference to me.

There are no bad guys in this story. Only, from my point of view, good people whose paths crossed in unfortunate ways. But I know one thing: Thomas does not belong in a cage.*

---

*Thomas served his sentence in state prison. Upon his release, he resumed drinking.

23

Bill Clune

My Marlboro Man, 2011

Bill Clune, unfiltered. Collection of Bill Kauffman.

I recently had lunch with my favorite model. Nah, not Cheryl Tiegs, pinup girl of many a 1970s lad, but Bill Clune, the fittest-looking 85-year-old since—well, since his dad, who lived to a hale 105.

Bill rode the whirlwind for a decade, from 1955 to 1965, as perhaps the highest-paid male model in America. He worked with the chichi photographers of the day: Irving Penn, Richard Avedon, Mark Shaw, Frank Scavullo (whom success renamed Francesco). Bill was television's first Marlboro Man, though he struck his cowboy pose sitting atop a split-rail fence in the Elliot Unger Elliot Studio on West Fifty-Fourth Street, five thousand martinis east of the lonesome prairie.

Bill had pedigree. His father, Henry W. Clune, was the star of Frank Gannett's Rochester newspaper and a novelist praised by the likes of Dawn Powell. His mother, Charlotte, daughter of adventurer Joe "King of the Klondike" Boyle, swam the 100-meter freestyle for the 1920 US Olympic team at Antwerp.

Their son, however, was floundering. He'd been fired from his weekend Rochester DJ job—spinning "Clune's Tunes"—after a mike caught him uttering mild profanities during a Mutual Network religious program. That was probably the last time Lady Luck rejected Bill Clune.

At loose ends in 1953, he climbed into his 1941 Ford and with $100 in his pocket drove to New York City. Reversing that tired Frank Sinatra song, Bill figured that if he couldn't make it in Rochester, he may as well take Manhattan.

A friend introduced him to John W. Harkrider, who had directed the 1929 Flo Ziegfield extravaganza *Glorifying the American Girl.* Harkrider, whom Bill remembers as a "nut box," got him a job posing as a rapist for Howell Conant in *True Detective.* Bottom's barrel was being scraped, but Bill was on his way. (So was Conant, who would be Grace Kelly's palace photographer.)

Soon, Clune's long-nosed handsome mug was all over the place: *Harper's Bazaar, Mademoiselle, Esquire, Vogue, Life, The Saturday Evening Post.* He had the outdoor look prized by Marlboro, which had been a lady's cigarette—its motto was "Mild as May"—until undergoing phalloplasty on Madison Avenue. (Bill was a stranger to the demon weed, so he spent the weekend preceding the Marlboro shoot gagging his way through a self-taught smoking tutorial.)

Hearst columnist Dorothy Kilgallen gushed, "Flicker scouts are excited about the male model of the moment—Bill Clune. He's the son of a Rochester newspaperman, and the experts think he may be another John Wayne."

Patrick Wayne was closer to the mark, though you can glimpse Bill as the coal-mine owner in Martin Ritt's cave-in *The Molly Maguires*.

Bill surveys his career with a charmingly wide-eyed wonder. Did he dislike anyone? "Dorian Leigh," he spits out, suggesting that the author of the autobiography *The Girl Who Had Everything* didn't. He also cites Millie Perkins, the New Jersey model who played the mysterious woman in Monte Hellman's 1967 cult western, *The Shooting*: "God she was nasty."

Bill bought the farm in 1958: a Greek Revival farmhouse and eighty acres in Livingston County, New York, where he raised ducks and pigs and cattle and chickens. On Saturdays, he and his wife would "hop in the car and go driving looking for real people because the rest of the week I was living in an unreal world."

Look magazine ran a four-page profile titled "The Double Life of a Farmer" in which Bill was depicted riding a tractor, oiling a hay cutter, sitting in a hayloft, and otherwise modeling the agrarian life. His wife was pictured aiming a .22 at something—maybe a woodchuck, but quite possibly at Bill, who was a chronically unfaithful husband. He lost the farm when he lost his wife.

Bill's friend Colin Fox, the British sailor who donned an eye patch as the Hathaway Shirt man, once was asked how people respond when they find out he's a male model. "Contempt," Fox replied. "This is usually followed by envy. They're thinking: 'Look at that conceited imbecile, making all that money just for smirking into a camera.' "

Yet Bill muses that his experience flip-flopped the stereotypes. Life on the farm is thought to be all honest toil and the world of high fashion a pit of glamorous decadence. But he greatly admired the work ethic of the best models and photographers, and he was puzzled to receive checks from Uncle Sam paying him for not growing corn or wheat. Sometimes the focus is hard to find.

Bill works still, his plummy voice much in demand for voice-overs. He's also peddling a memoir: the story of how Boy Scout virtues—be punctual, helpful, friendly—and a prodigious heterosexual appetite kept him plenty busy in the *Mad Men* age.*

---

*Bill never did sell that memoir. He died at the age of ninety-eight in November 2023.

24

Pat Weissend

Dead Presidents, 2024

Pat Weissend visits Herbert Hoover. Courtesy of patspresidentialplaces.com.

Where better to talk about dead presidents than over beer and wings at Jim's Saloon in East Pembroke, New York, three days before Millard Fillmore's birthday?

Across the table from me is Pat Weissend, a convivial bank manager and former museum director who has visited the grave sites of all thirty-nine dead presidents and all but two of the forty-three dead vice presidents of the United States. (The hard-to-get veeps are Walter Mondale, whose ashes have yet to be interred under the cold hard Minnesota ground, and Nelson Rockefeller, whose private and inaccessible burial spot is the Holy Grail of the grave-hunting community.)

We're chatting about twenty miles north of President Fillmore's old law office and an equal distance east of his remains in Buffalo's Forest Lawn Cemetery, whose primary tourist attraction is the headstone ("I've Had It All / I've Done It All / I've Seen It All / It's All About Love / God Is Love") of Rick "Superfreak" James.

Pat's interest in US presidents was sparked in his boyhood by little effigies his aunt gave him. I had the same set, which my grandmother bought president by president at Star Market circa 1970. Unlike Pat, I didn't try to decapitate mine by shooting rubber bands at their heads.

He took up his hobby in earnest in 1996, with visits to New Yorkers Martin Van Buren (Kinderhook) and Chester Arthur (Albany). He and his wife Peggy, Pat's equal in brio, cheer, and uproarious good humor, have since crisscrossed America, knocking off Oval Ones and second bananas and also-rans, typically on side trips from Kiwanis conventions.

As his target list of electoral-vote winners and losers shrunk, Pat added deceased New York governors. He's notched forty-five of the fifty-two and expects to nab about half of the holdouts, including Mario Cuomo, on an upcoming trek to the Vampire City.

In a fit of madness, Pat once considered canvassing every deceased cabinet member, but he regained his senses, and so he has yet to make the acquaintance of Commerce secretaries Luther Hodges (Eden, North Carolina) and Frederick Mueller (Grand Rapids, Michigan).

The grandest and gaudiest memorials, opines Pat, are dedicated to assassinated Buckeyes Garfield and McKinley, and the most modest (and out-of-the-way) is Calvin Coolidge's humble stone in Plymouth, Vermont. ("You'd never know it was his other than the presidential seal.")

Pat hasn't a morbid bone in his body, so why not birth places instead of resting places?

Because "some aren't there anymore," he says, instancing Rutherford Hayes, who came into this world on a piece of earth that is now a gas station.

A hunter's work is never done. Pat still has thirteen losing presidential candidates and fourteen losing vice-presidential candidates to go. They range from Nathan Sanford (Flushing, New York), Henry Clay's 1824 running mate, to George Wallace's 1968 bomb-happy partner Curtis LeMay (Colorado Springs, Colorado).

Trespassing is only a crime if you get caught. Pat has jumped fences in Oyster Bay, Long Island, to pay his respects to Teddy Roosevelt, and Timonium, Maryland, to bask in the spectral presence of Spiro Agnew. "I told the Roosevelt story on my website (www.patspresidentialplaces.com)," he says, "and the caretaker wrote, 'Trespassing is not funny. If I had caught you I'd have had you arrested.' "

Hey, sexton, TR the maniacal imperialist didn't respect boundaries, so why should Pat?

Woodrow Wilson, entombed in Washington, DC's National Cathedral, is typically one of the easiest dead presidents to find, but on Pat's first attempt the cathedral was hosting a memorial service for Princess Di and so was closed to the hoi polloi.

"C'mon," Pat's brother pled to a guard. "We just want five minutes."

"Not today," she replied. Brother Weissend, perhaps having seen too many movies, pulled a twenty from his wallet and dangled it before the stern sentry. She was, alas, incorruptible, at least at that price.

Pat finally nailed Wilson, the priggish maker of war and shredder of the Bill of Rights, a decade later.

Under my beery questioning Pat admits that he, like others in his fraternity, has the inevitable trip to Plains, Georgia, all mapped out. He figures that as long as he's in the neighborhood, he'll also knock off Herschel Johnson (Louisville, Georgia), running mate of Democratic candidate Stephen Douglas in 1860, and Fielding Wright (Rolling Fork, Mississippi), undercard on Strom Thurmond's Dixiecrat ticket in 1948.

Like any bucket list, there's always another item to cross off. And when there isn't? Well, those 600-plus cabinet secretaries are still waiting.*

*As this book went to press, Pat had a new dead president on his list (Jimmy Carter) but he'd cut the number of unvisited losing presidential candidates to ten.

25

Granville Hicks

Hicks's Town, 2005

Granville (not a hick) Hicks. Wikimedia Commons. National Portrait Gallery/ Clara Sipprell.

In 1932, Marxist literary critic Granville Hicks and his wife, Dorothy, bought an eight-room farmhouse in Grafton, New York, a rural hamlet ten miles east of Troy, where Hicks taught English to the young engineers at Rensselaer Polytechnic Institute (RPI). For three years, they lived as summer people, estivating intellectuals, divorced from the community. But when RPI fired Hicks for his Communist Party membership in 1935, he and Dorothy settled into Grafton for good—and for better, as it turned out. *Small Town* (1946), which Fordham University Press has republished in a handsome edition graced by an informative, sympathetic Introduction by Warren F. Broderick, is Granville Hicks's account of life in Grafton.

As a boy, Hicks had been something of a sissy, an unhappy New England Unitarian who "did badly in games." He was high school valedictorian, but his neighbors "knew that I would be out and away—like all the other bright boys of the towns and the smaller cities of America." He believed in science, reason, progress: the whole progressive shebang that would give us such marvels of the modern world as Hiroshima, Nagasaki, and metrication. Hicks was well on his way to peripatetic professorhood, a placeless existence in which he could theorize about the proletariat without actually having to meet any of it.

But Grafton interfered. "I wanted roots," he writes. He and Dorothy found their fixer-upper dream house on a dirt road just outside Grafton. Though Hicks was a "radical intellectual . . . , I took the same kind of pleasure in the ownership of property that my mother and father would have taken." Grafton did not undo Granville's communism: Hicks didn't even join the Party until he'd been in town for three years. But it refocused his leftism onto the human scale; it reinforced the anti-urban bias of the small-town boy; it taught him things quite beyond the ken of the *New Masses*.

To the bemusement of his urban friends, Hicks pledged his allegiance to Grafton. And the town accepted him. As Warren Broderick writes, Hicks was "viewed as a personable, harmless, overeducated eccentric" with offbeat political views. No one really cared that he was a communist, for as Hicks writes, in rock-ribbed Republican Grafton, "a communist seemed only slightly more dangerous and slightly more bizarre than a Democrat."

In time, Granville Hicks became a citizen. Grafton became his town. He was part of its daily life. He donated books that became the core of the Grafton Free Library. He edited a biweekly town newsletter. He helped establish the Grafton Fire Company and Grafton Elementary School. He served as a school-district trustee. He organized harvest dances, for which he also wrote skits. His wife was president of the PTA. He was not slumming or playing at quaintness; he came to belong to Grafton. He writes the following:

> I have learned to like trading in a store where I am known by name and can meet friends and swap gossip. I like knowing the storekeeper not only as a man behind a counter but also as a human being. I feel that I know what I am doing when I vote for or against men I have seen again and again in a hundred different situations, men I have talked with, men I have heard talked about. I like the old-timers, too, though they don't always like me, and I know they are no fools. Their talk gives the town a past, and sometimes it makes the smart city folks seem shallow. I find it good . . . that I am thrown with many types of men and not merely with intellectuals. In short, I like living in a small town.

Hicks does not pretend to be one of the boys. He never does get used to the incessant chatter about car engines. And he accepts the persistence of memory in Grafton: "A man who has lived here thirty or thirty-five years tells me that you can't become a naturalized citizen in less than a century." In a passage that still rings true in interstate-bypassed America, Hicks tells "the outsider bride of a young native, 'You can say anything you want to about us to anybody in town, but everybody else is somebody else's cousin.' "

Hicks the erstwhile progressive comes to doubt that rolling icon of the More Abundant Future, the automobile. ("[I]t speeded the decay of the community . . . a disintegrating force.") He searches Grafton in vain for class stratification, finding instead "a basic social equality that results from the smallness of the community and the sense of a common past." To his satisfaction, Granville Hicks learns that "in the small town you know everybody or nearly everybody, and . . . you know a considerable number of persons in a considerable number of ways." The man from whom you buy firewood is also a deacon in your church, his son is the point guard on the high school basketball team on which your son is a benchwarmer, and so on. By contrast, "the city dweller . . . rarely has intimate friends in any social or economic group but that to which he belongs."

City people, mere orts in the manswarm, cannot really know more than a tiny fraction of the men and women within their daily orbit. The rest must be reduced to a single dimension, so that real, live, complicated, flesh-and-blood people with distinct, unique histories are shrunk to fit inside the shorthand used by Henry Luce then, Rush Limbaugh now. Liberal. Religious nut. Red state. Blue state. The language dehumanizes the user as well as his or her quarry.

Hicks, like every man, has his limitations, some rather severe. He is humorless. His prose is serviceable but never sparkling. He is no more accurate a seer than the rest of us: For instance, he is particularly impressed by the unrealized potential in the exciting new field of . . . social studies! Also, a certain biliousness colors his discussion of local politics, though he concedes that "I couldn't get elected as dogcatcher." Hicks is no lachrymose sentimentalist. He gets impatient with his neighbors, disturbed by their "intense clannishness, suspicion of outsiders, hostility to new ideas, resistance to change"—which may be necessary defense mechanisms for a small place besieged by school consolidators, draft boards, Taylorized factories, and summer people whose opinions come from *The New Yorker*.

Yet Hicks would become something of an evangelist for the American small town. His old friends probably sniggered when he declared in a 1946 radio debate: "Whenever I am in New York City, I wonder how people can live without quietness and without clean, fresh air. I wonder, too, how they can stand the pressure of anonymous humanity. I know people as individual human beings. I don't like the bitter faces and the sharp elbows of the subway."

To Grafton, perhaps Granville Hicks was vexingly voluble, too articulate by half, resented for his extensive book learning (if privately disparaged for a "lack of common sense"), but, as is said of abrasive or unpopular citizens who sit on boards and organize meetings in all the Graftons of America, he did a lot for the town.

Now and then, Granville Hicks, having jettisoned the juvenile certitude of the ideologue, seems to throw up his hands: "I do not know what should be done to save [Grafton], much less the world."

Oh no, Hicks, you knew. Man, you lived it.

PLACES

26

The Oneidans

2023

John Humphrey Noyes, perfected? Public domain/Wikimedia Commons.

If ever I write a sex farce—the demand so far has been muted—I need only head east 150 miles and detour back 150 years to the Oneida community, the utopian experiment in free love that thrived from 1848 to 1880 before the colony's unorthodox sexual arrangements led to its collapse—and, in a characteristically American turn of events, its road to riches.

Headquartered in a sprawling Mansion House—open today to visitors of all carnal habits—Oneida was a cerebral nineteenth-century soap opera awash in high-minded American radicalism and directed by the brilliant and charismatic megalomaniac John Humphrey Noyes. As a Yale Divinity School student, Noyes had declared himself free from sin: a perfected Christian. This astounding heresy soon made him an ex–Yale Divinity School student.

Like many a young man with big dreams, Noyes married a girl whose family wealth compensated for her plainness. Her dowry enabled him to found the Oneida colony on the precepts of Bible communism (all property was held in common), Christian perfectionism (which released members from the obligation to obey every jot and tittle of the moral law), and—the teaching that made Oneida infamous—what Noyes called complex marriage.

Oneida attracted a mélange of accomplished young women, often of high station; idealistic young men; wandering mystics (some saintly, some touched); and a gaggle of eccentrics, lured perhaps by the promise of utopia but more likely by the prospect of bluestocking poontang.

Though not classically handsome, the tall and slender Noyes radiated erotic holiness. One Oneidan wrote: "I went to his room and told him I could do one thing, and that was to submit myself to him and look for his spirit to enter into me and fill me. . . . He is full of mercy and tenderness."

Noyes was not reluctant to have his spirit enter his sister Oneidans. The door to his modest room was always open to those who wished to drop by for cards or coitus.

To forestall a population explosion, and to save women from the pain of childbirth, Oneidans practiced—fitfully—"male continence," or withdrawal. Noyes wrote at length on the subject, though he still fathered thirteen children. (Sometimes—as Meat Loaf explained so histrionically in "Paradise by the Dashboard Light"—you slip up, in which case the offspring were raised communally.)

Sexual congress was voluntary; Oneidans were free to refuse propositions. A third party, usually an elder, would act as intermediary in prospective liaisons. The petitioner—typically male—would request conjugation; if the object of his desire were amenable, the adjudicator would decide yea or nay.

The young bucks grumbled about Noyes's doctrine of "Ascending Fellowship," which directed younger men to postmenopausal women and younger women to older men—most prominently John Humphrey Noyes, who seems to have taken a particular interest in these initiations. Harriet, his meal-ticket wife, was now but a "yoke-fellow."

(Among those who turned against Noyes was a University of Michigan dropout named Charles Guiteau, whose strangeness caused most if not all his propositions to the women of Oneida to be rejected. They gave him the nickname "Charles Get Out." In 1865, Guiteau left Oneida; sixteen years later he assassinated President James Garfield.)

Lovers who developed feelings of, well, love for others were accused of harboring "the marriage spirit." They were upbraided, often scaldingly, in the "mutual criticism" sessions to which Oneidans submitted in lieu of formal rules and regulations. Noyes exempted himself from mutual criticism—unless, he said, Jesus and Saint Paul were to show up and find his faults.

Snickering aside, one must credit the Oneidans, who numbered 300 at their peak, for possessing that nineteenth-century American urge for self-improvement. They studied Greek, astronomy, grammar, algebra, and music. They played croquet and baseball; they put on plays and concerts; they fled to the fields to pick strawberries or enjoy the spring sunshine. There was a genuine joy at Oneida that was absent in most ostensibly utopian colonies, yet there were poisonous jealousies, rancorous fights, and, underlying all, the complications and heartbreaks and absurdities inherent in complex marriage.

In 1879, despairing of the selfishness of the new generation, Noyes announced the end of complex marriage. A brief sexual free-for-all ensued, followed by a splurge of conventional marriages. Noyes hightailed it to Niagara Falls, Canada, just ahead of the authorities, who had been spurred on by Presbyterian ministers insisting he be arrested for sexual irregularities.

A year later, this Upstate New York experiment in Bible communism and free-ish love broke up—or, rather, it transmuted into a joint-stock corporation called the Oneida Community, Limited, which became the nation's leading manufacturer of silverware.

The weird old America's most outrageous and successful experiment in communism ended—in an orgy of moneymaking.

27

The Utica Club

2013

Eugene Nassar, bard of Utica. Wikimedia Commons/creative commons/Clover Mancuso.

Shortly after entering wedded bliss a quarter century ago, my wife, a Los Angelena, told me that she wanted to see two cities: Utica and Cleveland.

I, as is my wont, made her dreams come true.

This fall I had the good luck to revisit the literary capital of the Mohawk Valley twice in a matter of weeks. First I spoke at Utica College, under the aegis of the school's Ethnic Heritage Studies Center and the Alexander Hamilton Institute, in a celebration of Utica and her faithful literary son, Eugene Paul Nassar. Upstate New York literature maven Frank Bergmann and Hamilton College history professor Bob Paquette arranged the event, which afforded me the great pleasure of meeting Gene Nassar. (As a biographer of the Anti-Federalist Luther Martin, who despised the nationalist Hamilton and defended his murderer Aaron Burr, I got a real kick out of the Alexander Hamilton imprimatur.)

My other Utica venture was to pay homage at the Forest Hill Cemetery to Harold Frederic, novelist and bigamist, whose story "The Copperhead" I adapted for a film to be released this spring. Details—and Oscars, surely—to follow.

Every small American city deserves a Gene Nassar. Mr. Nassar grew up among the Lebanese Christians of East Utica. As an adult, he established himself as a noted scholar of such poets as Wallace Stevens and Ezra Pound, while remaining rooted in the old neighborhood as a professor at Utica College and historian of his city, which he loves, sins and blemishes too, with the ardor of a native son.

Utica was once a baseball rival of Batavia's in the New York–Penn League, and I like to think that the minor-league qualities of such cities—their intimate scale, the blending of the homely and the idiosyncratic, their unexpected tolerance of eccentricity—are the true soul of America. And of baseball. The majors are built on home runs and TV timeouts and $50 parking fees. To hell with 'em. To hell with the Empire, too.

The glory and richness of America come not from its weaponry or wars, which debase us as much if not more than the relentlessly vulgar and witless products rolling off the entertainment industry's assembly line. Rather, our numen is found in our regions, our little places, the unseen America beyond the ken of our placeless rulers.

A national culture exists only if fed by a thousand and one local, particularistic streams. American culture without Utica and her sister cities is . . . what? Ke$ha? Katie Couric? *Entertainment Tonight*?

William T. Coggeshall, state librarian of Ohio (and later a Lincoln bodyguard), explained three years before the War came that "It is not enough . . . that a national literature exists. It is required of a nation, which combines wide differences of characteristics, that each shall have its own representation. A Republic of letters may be a confederacy of individualities, [just as] a Republic in politics may be a confederacy of States."

Before any potent or meaningful decentralist political movement develops in this country, we're going to have to rediscover the places in which we live. We have to remember *why* we love our country—and the reason isn't that "We're Number One!" or that we can sprawl out on the couch chanting "USA! USA!" as the bombs drop and the televised chickenhawks cackle.

That isn't patriotism. It isn't even a parody of patriotism. It's an allegiance to . . . nothing.

America, the myth goes, is a land of perpetual motion, of restless pioneers striking out for the West, or in our time, of restive television addicts lighting out for Las Vegas, with the miniset in the SUV playing "Two and a Half Men" DVDs so that unlike the Joads, members of this fambly don't have to talk to one another. We are, supposedly, always moving, never stopping, consumed by what William Cullen Bryant called "the vain low strife that makes men mad."

And yet the best American writers—even those who follow their characters on rafts down the Mississippi, even those who write books titled *On the Road* or *You Can't Go Home Again*—are almost always attached to a *place*. Not a home page, but a real, individuated place that is different from any other place on earth: Sarah Orne Jewett in South Berwick, Maine. Sinclair Lewis in Minnesota. Wendell Berry in Henry County, Kentucky. Thoreau in Concord.

The regionalist impulse in American letters is greater now than at any time since the mid-1930s. Backwoods New England. Romantic North Dakota. East Utica. Writers are looking homeward. Standing on what they stand for, as Edward Abbey used to say. Only good can come of this. The Little America ain't dead yet.

28

A Syracuse Idyll

2022

Irish on top, for once. Wikimedia Commons/Doug Kerr.

I have my flaws, but I do know how to treat a lady. Five years ago, for our thirtieth anniversary, I took my wife to a nineteenth-century mental hospital. (We didn't check in.) This year, to celebrate her birthday, I showed her a traffic light—and as a lagniappe, we gandered at a clock, too.

It's not quite as quotidian as it sounds. Well, maybe it is, but now that I've got you on the line, let me tell you why we drove two hours to Syracuse, the Salt City, to inspect a pair of everyday sights.

First, the light. In 1925 or thereabouts, the city of Syracuse installed a traffic signal with green on top and red on bottom in the Irish neighborhood of Tipperary Hill. This was done at the behest of an alderman surnamed Ryan. A proud Paddy politico, apparently.

Some unimaginative bureaucrat—eccentricity is not a valued trait in traffic engineers—ordered the colors transposed to their usual positions. This annoyed the local gamins, who objected to British red surmounting Irish green.

The Hibernian youths registered their disapproval of green's demotion by regularly pelting the light with "Irish confetti," aka rocks. The authorities eventually tired of fixing the broken signal and gave in. As the excellent Upstate journalist Sean Kirst records, "Tipp Hill received the only traffic light in the nation where the green shines over red."

Ethno-vandalism had triumphed!

Lucine and I and our friends Chuck and Pat gazed at the upside-down light for what seemed a fitting period of time. Our vantage point was a little street-corner park with a statue of an Irish family. The bronze Dad is pointing out this marvel to Mom and their two kids. Although Junior has a slingshot in his back pocket, Pat thought it too cautious a depiction. Why not show the hooligan hurling the rock that KO'ed the red? I suppose Pat's reaction was predictable: her great-uncles were IRA men who were deported from the Emerald Isle to Australia in the 1920s. She still holds a grudge.

Chuck, a retired judge, suggested that if I drove through the red light I could plead colorblindness. I chose obedience to the law.

As if seeing the light weren't enough excitement for one day, our quartet drove a few blocks into the city's bustling Armory Square precinct to check out the perpetual twenty-four-second clock, a chronometric curiosity.

I had mixed feelings about this one.

The digital timepiece, rising from the sidewalk, "honors the rule that changed basketball and saved the National Basketball Association," in the slightly hyperbolic language of the clock's inscription.

The Syracuse Nationals were a charter member of the NBA. (In 1963 they would fast-break it to Philadelphia and become the 76ers.) Danny Biasone, owner of the Nats, is credited as the prime mover behind the rule that required teams to shoot the ball before twenty-four seconds had elapsed on each possession. This time constraint had its first run-through in an August 1954 scrimmage in Syracuse; by October, it was dictating the pace of every NBA game, as it still does nearly seven decades later.

Nats' general manager Leo Ferris devised the double-dozen limit by dividing the 2,880 seconds in a 48-minute NBA game by the 120 shots he believed proper to a contest. It was the tyranny of the slide rule.

But this was the mid-1950s, recall, when standardization flattened out the odd and the idiosyncratic. The crazy old America was being regimented by conscription, school consolidation, loyalty oaths, and the double whammy of urban renewal and highway construction, which would deface our cities and displace our people.

Pastoral rhythms were out; the rat race was in. Subjecting cagers to artificial time limits was very much in the spiritlessness of the age. Then again, I'm such a sports reactionary I probably would have argued against cutting the bottoms out of Dr. James Naismith's peach baskets.

The NCAA adopted the shot clock in 1985; over the years its duration in the college game has been reduced from forty-five to thirty seconds. Typically, high school basketball uses a thirty-second clock, though this varies by state. Gone are the glorious days of the languid point guard, the stop-and-smell-the-roses small forward, the stalling underdog, and the eight to four final score. Instead it's all run run run, shoot shoot shoot, hurry hurry hurry.

We didn't dally at the twenty-four-second clock. The bloodless bottom-liners who run the NBA wouldn't have wanted us to. I was wishing we could have conjured up those Irish delinquents of a century ago, handed them rocks, and let them have at it.

29

Armenians in the Falls

2022

A bumper sticker for Lucine Kauffman's town supervisor campaign. Collection of Bill Kauffman.

If ever I piss on the grave of an American it will be that of Robert Moses, the highwayman whose road-building and neighborhood-obliterating projects in New York City and New York State threw half a million people out of their homes, as Robert Caro estimated in his biographical masterpiece *The Power Broker*. To those who had the temerity to object to their ejection, the monster Moses hissed, "When you operate in an overbuilt metropolis, you have to hack your way with a meat axe. I'm just going to keep right on building. You do the best you can to stop it."

So it was with teeth gnashing that I drove down Robert Moses Parkway in the city of Niagara Falls, New York, en route to the annual Armenian festival at St. Hagop Armenian Apostolic Church.

The Niagara Falls themselves—though significantly altered by the hand and blasting tools of man—always inspire awe, contrary to Oscar Wilde's crack that "Every American bride is taken there, and the sight of the stupendous waterfall must certainly be one of the earliest, if not the keenest, disappointments in American married life."

But the city that shares a name with the nearby cataracts remains a source of utter befuddlement. How on earth can one of the world's great natural tourist attractions be bordered by hazardous waste sites and hideous Brutalist architecture and block after block of squatter-occupied crack houses? What the hell happened?

The short answer is decades of corruption, destructive urban renewal, and deference to bullying Magic Bullet proponents like Robert Moses and the disastrous 1960s mayor, an itinerant Boston University School of Theology–trained minister turned industrial public relations flack with the risible name E. Dent Lackey. Alas, the Magic Bullets of Moses, Lackey, & Company were aimed directly at the city's temple.

I don't much mind the carnival barker atmosphere conjured by images of the pre-urban renewed Niagara Falls, with its wax museums and forlorn hope dreamers scrambling for the loose buck. In retrospect, their vulgar schemes and garish designs—deplored by the likes of Frederick Law Olmsted—had a rascally Mark Twainish charm. My scorn is reserved for the politicians and developers, whose greed and power lust account for most of the villainy that wrecked modern American cities.

By the early 1960s, wrote Edmund Wilson in *Apologies to the Iroquois*, the city of Niagara Falls, erstwhile "aviary of honeymooners," had become "almost indistinguishable from Gary, Indiana."

Thank God St. Hagop still stands, an island of Armenian-American faith and culture in a sea of boarded-up houses.

Lucine, my wife, is half-Armenian, rather like Cher (nee Sarkisian) and Kim Kardashian, though with a higher IQ and a less pecunious mate. Her Armenian relatives are a delight, not least because they make the best food on the planet.

Lucine's late father rekindled my affection for William Saroyan and schooled me in the politics of the Caucasus. His ancestors, some murdered and other displaced by the Turkish genocide, settled in Syria. Vasken came to the United States in the 1950s, acculturating himself in the taverns of Milwaukee by watching Green Bay Packers games on TV and listening to the bar talk. A soccer player, he developed an appreciation for American football but retained an accent that was part Aleppo-bred Armenian, part Cypriot boarding school.

There is a significant cultural difference and tension between the diaspora Armenians of his and Saroyan's generations and the Soviet Armenians who came to this country after the dissolution of the USSR, but I leave its exploration to those at Ground Zero in Southern California.

The crowd at St. Hagop seemed distinctly old-school Armenian American. I saw only two Kardashian-imitating girls.

Of course Lucine and I headed straight for the grub.

The printed menu said that dinners were ten tickets each, and bottled waters one ticket per. I asked how much twenty-two tickets cost. "Twenty-two dollars," the woman said with a "Duh" tone, as if explaining matters to a simpleton who somehow had wandered in.

"*Odar*," my wife whispered to me, using the wonderfully piquant Armenian word for outsider.

"*Armo*," I replied.

Hey, I've been Armenian-adjacent for thirty-five years now, so I think I've earned the right to mutter a slurry demonym now and then.

Outside the social hall, the high-rise Seneca Niagara Casino blots the western horizon. We pass on the chance to lose money and instead drive around the urban renewal–decimated downtown streets. I wonder idly where the Niagara Falls Museum, owned by the family of my friend Sander Abramson, once stood before Robert Moses's goons razed it.

We drive out of town, passing the Robert Moses Niagara Hydroelectric Power Station. There's that word again: power. I'm with Henry Adams: "Power is poison."

30

The Roquers of Angelica

2023

Jim Gallman, the Michael Jordan of Roque. Photo by Lucine Kauffman.

Goose pulling is dead and gone, and lawn darts are on life support, but roque is alive and well and avoiding the roster of extinct sports thanks to the good folks of Angelica, an attractive village of fewer than 1,000 souls in the southwestern corner of New York State.

What's that: You've never heard of roque? Affix a *c* to its left and a *t* to its right and you have its sporting parent. Roque is a nineteenth-century American variation on the erstwhile European pastime of the leisure class. A hybrid of croquet and billiards, it is played on an oval-octagonal court of sand and clay with fixed wickets and hardwood boundaries off of which a player can ricochet shots. Its mallets, shorter than those used in croquet, are now either homemade or handed down from roquers past.

Roque enjoyed a brief vogue. It was a medal sport at the 1904 Olympics in St. Louis, where Americans swept the gold, silver, and bronze. (The only nonmedalist was also American.) Public courts appeared here and there in the 1930s, courtesy of the New Deal's Works Progress Administration, but it just never caught on—except in Angelica, where Angelican exceptionalism has preserved an old court and transmitted a love, or at least liking, of the game to generations on end.

So on the first weekend of every August, Angelica, which was named for Alexander Hamilton's sister-in-law, Angelica Schuyler Church, hosts a roque tournament in its village park during "Heritage Days."

Amid craft vendors and Amish bakers and singers belting out classic country tunes, the only roque tournament in the world proceeds at an unhurried pace.

Jim Gallman, seventy-eight, is Angelica's tender of the roque flame. You can catch him every Tuesday morning at 9 a.m. as he booms "Good morning, Angelica!" over community radio station WRAQ 92.7 FM.

How long has Jim been playing roque?

"Since after the Civil War." He waits a beat. "Of course today is after the Civil War, too."

Jim took up the mallet in the 1950s, and while "the tremors" have sidelined him, he keeps close watch on the action from his courtside chair. Jim tried to explain the game's byzantine rules to me, but that effort was as hopeless as elucidating particle physics to a TikTok teenager. Basically, you thwack the ball through a series of iron arches, using the walls if necessary, and eventually you hit the home peg. A best-of-three match between two-person teams might take ninety minutes.

A healthy percentage of the thirty or so area roquers are Jim Gallman–adjacent. "There's my brother," he says, pointing to one player. "This is my son-in-law. That's my cousin's son." And so on.

The last rule book was published by the long-defunct American Roque League circa 1960. (It wistfully—or delusionally—called roque "the game of the century.") Jim tells me that someone once showed him a copy, but the rules didn't correspond with those handed down by tradition in Angelica, so the locals ignored it.

"We're interested in how *we* play, not how *they* played," he states with admirable firmness.

That's the spirit. Angelica Rules!

Jim Gallman has never seen another roque court, though press reports indicate that there may be private courts in Stuart, Florida, and on Cape Cod. I hope they play by similarly localized rules.

The players are competitive but peaceable. I saw no fights. Yet the two most prominent mentions of roque in popular culture are blood-stained.

In John Steinbeck's unheralded novel *Sweet Thursday* (1954), the neighboring communities of Monterey and Pacific Grove, California, come to blows over a tournament, leading to the discovery of one unfortunate who is "found clubbed to death with a roque mallet in the woods."

Stephen King, in *The Shining* (1977), has Jack Torrance explain the game to his wife and son, the Red Rum tyke. ("It's a little bit like croquet, only you play it on a gravel court that has sides like a big billiard table instead of grass.") Jack praises the hardness of the mallet with which he later tries to beat his wife to a pulp.

Stanley Kubrick's 1980 film adaptation discarded the roque mallet, substituting a ho-hum axe.

Every detail of Kubrick's horror masterpiece has been parsed by obsessives, so I ask the Room 237 crowd: What did the old boy have against roque? Did operatives of the American Roque League get to him? Or was he respecting Angelica's uniqueness, keeping its secret safe from the world?

31

The Schope Must Go On

The Chautauqua Institute, 2019

The Chautauqua Athenaeum, always improving. Wikimedia Commons.

When our friend the avant-garde playwright asked my wife to appear in his latest production, Lucine didn't realize she was going to have to make her own abacus. No, she wasn't playing Cleopatra's accountant, but rather the modern chatelaine of a resort hotel on the shores of New York's Chautauqua Lake, whose very name is redolent of uplift, of sedulous self-improvement, of the earnest aspirational Protestantism of the nineteenth-century Chautauqua movement—"the most American thing in America," as Theodore Roosevelt called it—whose spirit lives on in the nearby Chautauqua Institution.

Lucine and her castmates wore togas. (Don't ask why; I don't know.) The slippage of one actor's toga led to a wardrobe malfunction, à la Janet Jackson in the 2004 Super Bowl halftime show. The woman sitting next to me, whom I had met just minutes before, whispered urgently, "This may be too much information, but I can't take my eyes off that man's nipple." I nodded commiseratively, sipped my coffee, and stared at the table.

Oh, and before I get to the Lesson to be Drawn from this Experience, I should mention that the play also featured a teenaged girl dressed as young Arthur Schopenhauer reading passages of and glosses on the doleful Danziger's impenetrable prose. One memorable line began "Ontologically speaking . . ."

Meanwhile, my wife wandered the coffee house stage, shaking her head vigorously and muttering "poodles, poodles, poodles," which in my lowbrow enthusiasm I urged her to phrase in the way that Goober, cousin of television's Gomer Pyle, had intoned "Judy, Judy, Judy" when doing his Cary Grant imitation. Lucine's actorly instincts, as usual, were superior to mine. (With a few clicks of this infernal machine upon which I am typing we learned that Schopenhauer said that he preferred the company of poodles to "common bipeds," so literary-mystery solved.)

You will not believe me when I say truthfully that it all came off just fine, a strange and wonderful production, despite the penultimate scene, a Japanese tea ceremony so interminable that the clocks ran backward.

Nothing quite like the magic of live theater, eh? Men's nipples! A "sez who? Sez me" duet set to Schubert's *Trio Op. 100*! Arthur Schopenhauer gags!

To get in the mood, as it were, we visited the Chautauqua Institution a week before the show went up. Earnest lectures on the Issues of the Day were being delivered, consciences were being examined for Bad Thoughts, red MAGA hats and people who work as milkers or cashiers or blacktoppers were nowhere in sight. We were mainlining mainline Protestantism. As we walked the winding avenues, past million-dollar summer homes, a middle-aged man aglow with edification greeted us. "We're having talks this week about white privilege!" he burbled.

"That's appropriate," said my wife, surveying the grounds.

(Yes, the man really did say this—I could almost hear the strains of "Venus in Furs" as I pictured him squealing ecstatically while a well-compensated and Ivy-credentialed Person of Color scourged his pale flesh with hot words of reproach.)

We fled Chautauqua for the long ride home.

We hadn't time on this excursion into southwestern New York State to drop by neighboring Lily Dale, which also figured into the play. Lily Dale is the venerable spiritualist colony in which no one ever dies, or if they do they can be rung up on the spectral hotline for $100 an hour by a middling medium.

Schopenhauer Meets Chautauqua is *exactly* what the theater world needs now: homegrown, grassroots, locally accented plays that bring to life the idiosyncratic America that Taylor Swift and Netflix and the Department of Homeland Security would bury under the rubble of plastic and paranoia.

A pertinent pathetic story: In 2009, Rocco Landesman, President Obama's chairman of the National Endowment for the Arts, visited Peoria, Illinois, that Middle American metonym. The purpose was to demonstrate the vitality of theater in the heartland. How did Peoria demonstrate said vitality? Perhaps with a play about native son Richard Pryor, or a fantasia on the farm equipment industry, or some punked-up medley of the mellow tunes of Peoria's own Dan Fogelberg?

No. The community theater entertained him with a performance of *Rent.* How obediently they lapped up their betters' sloppy seconds!

The Peorians demonstrated their colonial servility, their abject and imaginationless acceptance of Mordor's culture-widgets.

Ontologically speaking, they dead. The poodles, however, keep on barking.

32

Shorty Doesn't Live Here Anymore

1997

Good, Good LeRoy Town. Photo by Lucine Kauffman.

The nearby village of LeRoy—pronounced La-Roy by its residents; and Leee-Roy, as in Selmon or Jordan, by the rest of us—is a gold mine of nicknames. Its leafy streets are populated by characters like Pickle, Boomer, Weegie, and my favorite, the late great Mr. "Eggs" Bacon.

But a fissure has developed. The interstate, that human conveyor belt and model of government-subsidized mobility, opened a LeRoy exchange some years ago, and Rochester yuppies who didn't mind a half-hour commute could purchase their own little piece of quaintness. An unpalatable cleft resulted, and nowhere is this more evident than in the use of sobriquets. Old-time LeRoyans (including several relatives of mine) still traffic in nicknames, but the newer folk, for the most part, do not. It's not that they don't want charming monikers hung 'round their necks, it's just that they haven't earned them. For most nicknames attach themselves in childhood and are not portable: Abandon the scene of your boyhood and bid farewell to Tiny, Tim.

To acquire a nickname is easy; to maintain one is harder, as it requires continuous residence in one place. This is why almost no one in the transient quarter of Washington, DC, has a nickname—except for manufactured or self-applied ones, such as the absurd "Comeback Kid" that Bill Clinton hung on himself.

The same is true in sports. We hear laments that nicknames have disappeared from the pros—Rube and Mudcat and Duckie have given way to, at best, such infelicitous media inventions as "The Big Hurt" or "Mr. October." (Can you imagine addressing a friend in so stilted a manner? "Hey, The Big Hurt, let's grab a beer.")

In our town we have had a minor-league baseball team for nearly sixty years—the Class A Batavia Clippers—and while our current overlords, the Philadelphia Phillies, seldom send us the Moose Kromkos and Sneaky Gradys of yesteryear, the players are merely the supporting cast anyway. The richness, the continuity, the meaning is supplied by the fans, and the thousand and one nights we have shared, in chilly Junes and dying Augusts.

My father was a Clippers batboy in the 1940s, and from him I have learned of the pepper-pot second baseman who'd yell, "Whaddaya want, egg in yer beer?" to picky hitters. (When dad tried that on his mother, he got a bar of soap in his mouth.) Young and old alike know about the night of the dense fog a half-century ago, when the right fielder carried a ball out to his position each inning until finally a visiting batter knocked one over the cloud-shrouded right-field wall, and the right fielder taught the impressionable youth of Batavia how to really rob a home run.

I am passing on this lore to my daughter, who is barely three. She sits with me in the bleachers, as I once sat with my family. (And, once, our knight in shining catcher's pads—Dave Bike, where are you?—who, after getting tossed from a game for using a hoary epithet, came up and sat with us in the stands, just us kids, and bought us pop and hot dogs. How rare the twenty-year-old player who has the wisdom to understand what this means to children.)

I also take my daughter to Batavia High football games. We sit briefly on a rickety bleacher on the visitors' side, where the embittered ex-jocks sit, cursing the coach's play calling and the referee's sight. But let the spectator's third cousin make a block on a punt return and it's whooping and hollering and "waytago Jimmy!" and high-fives all around. At the games I see timeless friends and the older boys (nicknamed all) who walked as giants when I was young—the quarterback who went away to college and came back a lawyer, the good-time Charlie who became a cop, the faded jock who nightly replays his broken-field touchdown run on a barstool.

The paunch advances as the hairline retreats, and someday I will be like my grandmother, who makes almost weekly trips to the funeral parlor to say goodbye to friends she has known for eighty-plus years. Teachers in rural schools speak of the comforting sense of familiarity that long years in one place can bring: Pretty girls beget pretty girls, just as the wild boys and their police-blotter antics are renewed with each generation. The names and faces remain the same; only the hair lengths change.

With shared memory and the mythicization of the everyday, our lives take on meaning. The alternative is a life lived on the edge of the abyss. We lose ourselves in crowds, yet a terrible fear of anonymity haunts many Americans. We want to be known, remembered, thought of, and this is only possible in small communities and networks of families. Those cut off from such possibilities are driven to freakish acts of exposure, such as appearing on "Jenny Jones" or "Meet the Press."

Yet external pressures conspire to drive us away from the familiar, toward the abyss. Consider a pair of colloquialisms. "He'll go far," approving elders say of promising youngsters, with the implication that success can be measured in the distance one has traveled from home. If, on the other hand, we say of a boy, "He's not going anywhere," we are not praising his steadfastness but damning him as an ambitionless sluggard. Absence may make the heart grow fonder, but love's greatest demand is immobility.

Our hollows aren't sleepy enough; but then, they've never been. Even Washington Irving complained, "There is no encouragement for ghosts in most of our villages, for they have scarcely had time to finish their first nap and turn themselves in their graves before their surviving friends have traveled away from the neighborhood; so that when they turn out at night to walk their rounds they have no acquaintance left to call upon."

Last fall our county historical society was wracked by that bane of all thoughtful people everywhere—divisiveness. For the first time in over a century, the presidency was contested. As we finished our pork chops and got down to the messy business at hand, a nice young community college instructor who had just moved here from Brooklyn, 400 miles away, stood up and said, "How can we vote on candidates if we don't know anything about them? Can't they each give a two-minute speech or something?" He was greeted by a gust of good-natured boos. He sat, bemused and embarrassed. A woman kindly explained to him, "But you see, we do know them. Everyone knows everyone else. They don't have to say anything." Speeches, and the webs of dissimulation the glib can weave, were unnecessary. We knew the character, the background, the families of the candidates, and so, unlike the votes we cast every four years for the unidimensional TV creatures who would be president, we marked our ballots with confidence. The result was a landslide.

"Restoring civil society" is the Next Big Issue among the rootless PhD's and hyperkinetic politicians of America—men and women who have "gone far." But civil society is that historical society meeting, as it is also spinster librarians compiling town histories in self-published books, volunteer firemen and bingo callers (often one and the same), and the boys slugging 'em down at the St. Nick's Club. Intellectuals who push "civil society" on these folks are about as convincing as Jimmy Swaggart lecturing an eighty-three-year-old virgin in Shreveport on the virtue of chastity.

A few months back, I caught one of the civil society gurus on television, their true and only milieu. How happily I clicked off his scowling face. For it was a glorious October morning, when I walk with my wife and daughter through the park trod as a boy by my father, and his father before him. My daughter collects chestnuts that drop from the trees that supplied me and my brother. That she will do the same with her children, and they with theirs, sustains me. For as the great-grandmother tells the boy Douglas in Ray Bradbury's *Dandelion Wine*, "No person ever died that had a family."

33

Ten Years After a Place in Time

2013

"When I paint my masterpiece . . ." © Henry Holt.

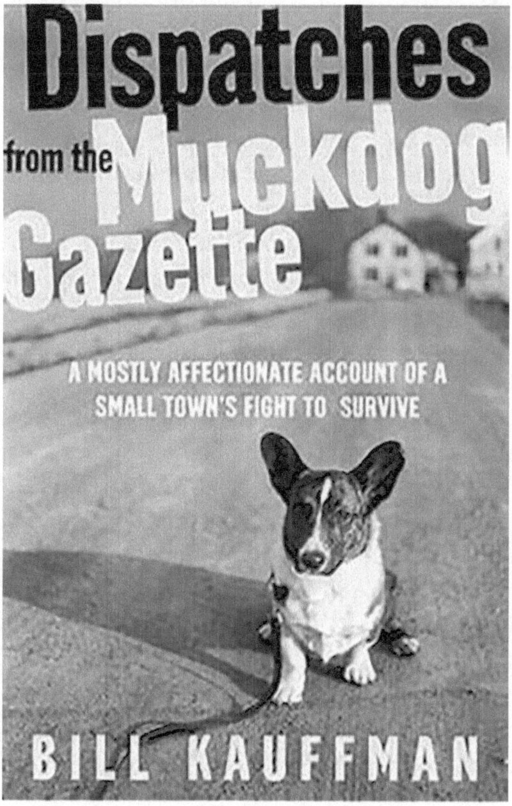

Thomas Wolfe, the adjectival Tar Heel, not the dandified Virginia expositor of *The Right Stuff,* philosophized in his execrably titled *You Can't Go Home Again* that "A man learns a great deal about life from writing and publishing a book."

He can say that again . . . and again. (I'll always love Wolfe, who meant a great deal to me when I was younger, but one of my favorite stories about the logorrheic author is that he prefaced the manuscript that became *Look Homeward, Angel* with an assurance that "I do not believe the writing to be wordy, prolix, or redundant.")

March 2013 marks the tenth anniversary of the simultaneous launching of the Iraq War and my memoirish tale of going home again (and what I found there), *Dispatches from the Muckdog Gazette.*

I guess there just wasn't enough space in the American attention span to accommodate both these events, so despite the best efforts of the good folks at Henry Holt, shock and awe hogged all the headlines. Those bastards Bush and Cheney—what infernal timing they have!

I did, however, learn a bit about life from that experience.

Honesty is not just the best but the only policy for a writer. As Thoreau counseled, "Say what you have to say, not what you ought. Any truth is better than make-believe." Given that this book's subject was my hometown of Batavia, New York, there was no way to be honest without bruising feelings. To have been cautious or solicitous would have caused severe anemia and crashing boredom.

A month or so before publication I came down with the usual auctorial premonitions of disaster. There was a good deal of anticipation around town surrounding publication, to which my reaction was "Holy Crow—people here are actually going to *read* this." What, I wondered, was the modern equivalent of being run out of town on a rail?

For in *Dispatches,* I treated with wit (half-wit, if you don't like it) and gleeful scatter-sprayed invective the ethno-religious conflicts that once rived—and, in a way, fortified—my town. As a typical American mongrel, with mixed bloodlines and a shambling sympathy for all sides of the American divide, I claimed an exemption from oppressive sensitivity codes. I wrote about the faded WASP ruling class from the point of view of the once-déclassé Italian and Irish Catholics, and I wrote about the latter from the POV of the former. After all, I'm dago, mick, limey, kraut, papist, Prot . . . that's a pretty wide free-fire zone.

Wolfe described "with bitter chagrin" the reception of *Look Homeward, Angel* (1929) by his hometown of Asheville, North Carolina. The vitriol fell like acid rain. But then Wolfe had fled North Carolina for exile in New York City.

He wrote of a tormentor: "One venerable old lady, whom I had known all my life, wrote me that although she had never believed in lynch law, she would do nothing to prevent a mob from dragging my 'big overgroan karkus' across the public square."

I heard through the grapevine of—mercifully few—people who were offended by my Italian jokes. (My Stella lineage provided insufficient protection—but then my grandmother always said we were "northern Italian, almost Swiss.") From the other side, I was taken to task by the octogenarian grande dame of our city, who had grown up in presprawl Long Island and still sounded like it.

She confronted me after a concert at St. James Episcopal Church. "I'm baaah-lee speaking to you," she announced.

Wolfe-like, I had known my venerable critic since I was a boy. She taught me to swim. I threw my hands up in mock surrender.

"Sorry . . . sorry," I stammered, certain that I knew the source of her displeasure: my raillery about upper-crust Protestants.

"How *could* you say that I have an ox-cent?" she asked in her inimitable accent.

I laughed. "Is that all?"

"Yes. And why must you use so much profanity?"

I acknowledged my literary Tourette's. Within the month she was speaking to me again. As I write this she is 92 and we're still pals. (Catherine Roth, the grande dame, died in April 2020 at the age of 101. I occasionally edit while sitting on her memorial bench in the Old Batavia Cemetery.)

Various outlets sold upward of 800 copies of the book in Batavia—an extraordinary number for a rural working-class burg of 15,000 souls. As for sales in the rest of the good old USA . . . I blame Bush.

I had used as an epigraph this line from Sinclair Lewis's *Cass Timberlane*: "To its fugitive children, Grand Republic will forgive almost anything, if they will but come back home."

You *can* go home again. And if they'll forgive me, they'll forgive anyone.

34

Thirty Years After a Place in Time

2020

How it began. © Soho Press.

The thirtieth anniversary of the publication of my first and only novel, *Every Man a King*, has passed, so I guess the trigentennial *festschrift* must have fallen through. Shucks. These decennial let-downs are enough to make a man doubt the existence of Google. But *Moby Dick* wasn't squeezed into the canon until the centenary of Herman Melville's birth, so I got nothin' but time.

I had, in manuscript, called the novel *Fortunate Son*, after that chugging anthem of defiance and resentment by Creedence Clearwater Revival, but the legendarily nurturing editor Laura Chapman Hruska of the great Soho Press retitled it *Every Man a King*, from the splendidly equalitarian slogan of the rantipole 1930s Louisiana populist Huey Long, for whom I have a very soft spot despite his, shall we say, flaws.

I cringe now to recall the great expectations surrounding the book's parturition. I had wanted my first (presumptuous adjective!) novel to be published when I was twenty-eight or twenty-nine, as was the case with Sinclair Lewis, Frank Norris, Thomas Wolfe, Jack Kerouac, and others whose company I aspired to keep. I was also under the spell of *Crumbling Idols* (1894), Hamlin Garland's stirring if long-forgotten manifesto of populist regionalism, with its emphatically italicized conclusion that "*Provincialism (that is to say, localism) is no ban to a national literature*."

Oh, I was bound for glory, all right. My ever-indulgent aunt, Jane (never "Aunt Jane"—that made her sound old), suggested that my family take "coping lessons" in order to deal with my impending fame. These proved quite unnecessary, and in the three decades since, my master plan to avoid fame and fortune has worked to perfection.

Upon receipt of my box of author's copies, I marched over to the house in which I grew up and presented a signed book to my parents. All that early promise . . . redeemed! My mother opened it, began reading, and upon reaching a rather too explicit sex scene within the first six pages she burst into tears. My hurried protestations that I knew nothing of such matters and had only heard about them from "some guy" were unavailing. The plot concerned a boy from the sticks of Upstate New York who briefly shines in Washington before an unforgivable televised slip of the tongue chases him back home, where he must live among the common folk he had, in exile, idealized. The novel was in no wise autobiographical, but I learned to my discomfort that all fiction is assumed to be thinly disguised, if occasionally embellished, memoir. I had to spend a solid year assuring readers that I did not prematurely ejaculate. Boy was that ever embarrassing. And Laura, my preternaturally wise editor, once asked my wife over the phone, "Are you Wanda?"—a reference to the slattern with whom the protagonist takes up. Yikes!

Prepublication trade reviews were quite good, and commercial hopes skyrocketed when Soho learned that Jonathan Yardley, then the nation's leading book reviewer, was featuring it in *The Washington Post.* Alas, Yardley adjudged the first half of the book sparkling satire, the second half soggy sentiment. So much for an Emersonian "I greet you at the beginning of a great career" blurb. But that's us localists: sodden simpering saps. In any event, the book was commercially DOA. Like Delmore Schwartz, I had a blind date with reality. Into the hands of discerning posterity do I commend my novel.

Still, it's had an afterlife, however wraith-like.

When a movie producer called to inquire about a collaboration, I brushed him off as if I were Henry James and he were a patent medicine salesman asking me to write copy for his liver pills. What sort of money-grubbing middlebrow vulgarian do you take me for, sir?!

A decade or so later, my friend Peter Dzwonkoski, then-director of Rare Books and Special Collections at the University of Rochester library, invited Jonathan Yardley to speak at the university upon the appearance of *Misfit* (1997), his biography of my fellow Upstater Frederick Exley, whose papers Peter had purchased. Peter thought it might be fun to introduce critic and wronged writer. I suppose if I'd been some 1920s drunken dukes-up made-wiser-by-my-experience-in-the-Great-War poseur I'd have made a gin-soaked scene. But I'm an admirer of Yardley's and a forgiving sort. Hey, we all have off days.

Long after its publication and disappearance into Remainder Valley, the *New York Sun* proclaimed *Every Man a King* the best political satire of the twentieth century, but the *Sun,* as suns will do, soon set.

So now, trudging across that long desert that separates *enfant terrible* from *eminence grise*—a friend of saturnine disposition says it's called "les miserables," but he would say that—I look forward to the quadragennial celebration in 2029. I'm sure I can dig up those coping lessons somewhere.

35

Moon Java

Satellite of Love, 2019

Batavia, New York, my favorite place in the world, was described by Alexis de Tocqueville on his American tour: "Scattered houses then marshes. Rooms built of tree trunks."

Okay, it wasn't the Frenchman's most memorable passage.

But at least Tocqueville was more charitable than my landsman John Gardner, the twentieth-century novelist, who called Batavia a symbol of "both spiritual death and the death of civilization."

Ouch!

Gardner, a nomadic academic who had left town years earlier, was responding to the razing of Batavia's core in the 1960s with federal money from the cruelly misnamed urban renewal program, an act of wanton destruction—desecration—which I suppose explains why I abhor grandiosity, men who Dream Big, and those who worship the noun *change*. Not that Washington, DC, bears all the blame for this municipal homicide. For it was suicide, too, as our city fathers, bedazzled by the goddess Progress, were complicit. But it's a fallen world, and what can we do but forgive, forgive, and then forgive some more? (I used to want to string those responsible from a lamppost, but I've mellowed in late middle age.)

I sit writing this and gobbling down a raspberry scone in Moon Java, a marvelously unpretentious coffee shop and gathering place tucked in the quondam Massey-Harris farm equipment factory. I stare across the street at the Old Batavia Cemetery, wherein I will dwell someday—some distant day, I trust. Or at least my mortal remains will there repose, while my spirit dawdles in the bus station called Purgatory.

In the distance I spot the obelisk of Joseph Ellicott, our town's founder, who in 1826 hanged himself in an insane asylum, leaving a suicide note that whined, "However much I give to people, they do not love me."

I promise not to burke myself, and I sure won't leave any self-pitying valedictory, though all you bastards out there who never bought my books will have to answer to a higher power, and I don't mean Jeff Bezos.

This small city (population 15,012) of my birth, which is more or less conterminous with my imagination, is the seat of rural Genesee County at the western edge of that section of Upstate New York once known as the Burned-Over District, an appellative nod to the nineteenth-century fires of idealism and kookery that scorched these parts: anti-Masonry, Mormonism, feminism, Shakerism, abolitionism. (I leave the idealism/kookery distinctions to the reader.) Fires damped, we are now a punched hole in the Rust and Opioid Belt. The county went for Donald Trump by a margin of better than two-to-one, not because many were taken in by his carnival-barker bombast but because, unlike the submissive helpmeet of Wall Street and the perpetual-war complex whom the Democrats nominated, Trump did not obviously hate our guts.

I am a part of this place, indissolubly, and it is a part of me; as my fellow Upstater Frederick Exley, the bibulous memoirist of *A Fan's Notes*, once said of his hometown, "Watertown is not *in* my marrow; it *is* my marrow." On Upstate's flipside, Michael Bennett, director-choreographer of *A Chorus Line*, cracked of his natal place, "To commit suicide in Buffalo is redundant." But Exley was a sensitive artist and Bennett a coke-fiend Broadway schlockmeister with about as much soul as a Times Square souvenir kiosk, so there.

The necrotic effects of cable television on the tissues of civic and social life are much less advanced here than in the metropoles. One needn't enlist in the cretin armies of Sean Hannity or Rachel Maddow. Intimacy of scale means that like and unlike are thrown together in community enterprises. I have seen Assembly of God church elders work side by side with very out gays in the cheerful labor of neighbors because they come to know each other as rounded, multidimensional persons. This is simply not possible on a mass scale, or with TV or the internet as intermediary. Genuine *diversity*, that formerly useful word that has been drained of all meaning, exists at the human scale but is a grotesque parody on a larger stage. It has ever been so: there was an infinitely greater diversity of thought in a 1912 meeting of the Burdett, Kansas, chapter of the Woman's Christian Temperance Union than there is today in the entirety of the Manhattan and Brooklyn art scene.

The older I get the more it all seems like a vivid and continuous dream, to borrow a phrase from John Gardner. Which returns us to forgiveness, for despite our status as civilization's terminus, every October, twenty or so of us gather at Gardner's favorite diner, the Pok-a-Dot, to read from his works and conjure his troubled spirit. *Je me souviens*, in the wonderful motto of Quebec. I remember; we remember.

Batavia is the birthplace and only surviving charter member of the Class A New York–Penn League, and like the thousand-plus minor-league baseball games I have witnessed since childhood this place is comfortingly familiar—until, that is, a beanball knocks you down, or an audacious kid steals home. And so a boyhood friend, recently released from prison, tears up as he recalls the pickup football games of our youth; bright-eyed little girls are reduced by heroin and hopelessness to ashes in urns; the town skinflint commits furtive acts of generosity.

The dream herks and jerks its way unto the next chapter.

My friend Henry W. Clune, an underrated Rochester novelist who died at the Methuselan age of 105, used to say that all he ever really wanted was to appear considerable in the eyes of his hometown. I'll settle for staying out of the police blotter. But no place on earth will ever appear as considerable to me, as full of meaning and mysteries that I will never quite puzzle out, as my hometown.*

---

*Moon Java closed in 2020, a COVID casualty. Its successor, Pub Coffee Hub, shuttered in 2024. I am undercaffeinated.

36

In This House that I Call Home

2021

All (well, a lot of) our memories are there. Collection of Bill Kauffman/Painting by Patricia Burr.

"Property is proper to man," said Dorothy Day, and if *home*—its protection, its cultivation, and love thereof—is the cynosure of any healthy political movement, I may as well tell you about mine. About *ours*.

We bought this modest 1830s Greek Revival (which hadn't indoor plumbing until the 1980s) in 1992 off Gabby, who, bless her heart, had rescued it from demolition. The divorced wife of a banker, she was European, sensual, a soi-disant "artist"—an exotic in these parts. We were told that she glided around the sheerly curtained house in the nude. I expect the men of our street were sad to see her go.

Gabby had painted the house in pinks and pastels and dubbed it La Maison des Fleur Printemps, making it the only abode in the county with its own name tag on a shingle.

The springtime lilacs, tulips, and dandelions are lovely, to be sure. (I hold with James Russell Lowell that those common golden flowers, the last-named of that trio, "art more dear to me / Than all the prouder summer-blooms may be.") But about forty-five seconds after we moved in, I ripped that damned sign out of the ground. I'm about as Franco-American as SpaghettiOs. A paint job in sunshine yellow soon followed.

The former chatelaine, a devout believer in the healing power of crystals, had lodged miniature glass talismans in every nook and cranny of the *maison*. She also told us that "pixies and fairies" frolicked in the flower beds out back. I've seen a few boozing it up in our kitchen now and then, but as far as I know they've left the flowers unmolested.

Nor have I espied the "beautiful white ghost" that Gabby claimed descended the stairs in the wee hours. The first night my wife and I spent in the house we slept on the living room floor. At about 3 a.m.—the soul's midnight, as Ray Bradbury called it—Lucine shook me awake.

"I think I see it," she whispered.

My first instinct, of course, was to feign deep slumber. Not for me this "I ain't afraid of no ghost" bluster. But upon investigation the specter was revealed to be the headlights of a vehicle coming 'round the bend.

I felt none of the smug satisfaction of the rationalist debunker. À la Russell Kirk, I wish the ghosts were real. For visitants we have to make do with the chittering chipmunks who squeeze into the walls on cold rainy nights.

If any house in town is wraith-ridden it ought to be ours. For perhaps half its life it was tenanted by the leading spiritualist family of Genesee County, which is near the western terminus of what the novelist-folklorist Carl Carmer called America's "psychic highway." True believer or humbug, credulous dupe or ectoplasmic evangelist, itinerant communers with the dead who passed through our county in the early twentieth century usually boarded with the Slaters.

The last of the line, the Madeline Usher of Chapel Street, was a purse-poor grimalkin with long coarse white hair. The kids of the neighborhood called her a witch, though I suspect she was merely shy and odd, one of those love-cracked solitaries sketched with such sympathetic observation by the great forgotten portraitist of eldritch spinsters, Mary Wilkins Freeman.

Miss Slater committed that gravest sin of mean old ladies: she kept the baseballs, footballs, and whiffle balls that landed in her yard. To be fair, the urchins were not blameless in this war. "We used to throw dogshit at her door," one gray hair confessed. Thankfully that practice died out with its victim.

As a rest-in-peace offering, I leave a token on the Slater gravestone in the cemetery through which I walk almost every day. It's a safer way to communicate than a seance.

I don't suppose we'll ever sell this nameless place—hey, it's home. So last year I relented in the decades-long argument with my wife over the paving of a driveway. "Why do our cars need a carpet?" I asked. Now they have one.

The looming battle is over a garage. "Why do our cars need a shrine?" I ask. We'll see how long I can hold out.

In the meantime I sit in the twilight, looking out over fields of corn or cabbage. I don't even mind the song that plays on the radio.

Don't have much money, but boy if I did
I'd buy a big house where we both could live

It's not that big, but you can't beat the *fleurs* every *printemps.**

---

*In 2025, after thirty-three years in the former La Maison des Fleurs Printemps, Lucine and I moved into the Batavia house my grandfather built in 1938. Not a day goes by that I don't think of our Elba home.

37

The Empire Versus Our Town

A Speech to the Fox Hill Bruderhof Community of Walden, New York, May 4, 2018

The Bruderhof: Antidote to Empire. Photograph by Danny Burrows, © Plough Publishing House, 2020. Used by permission.

Thank you for the invitation. I've been reading *Plough* with great avidity and I'm delighted to be here sharing the stage with my friend Patrick Deneen.

I come from the other end of the state, in Genesee County, which is one of the four New York counties with more cows than people. (I had a rather more than kin but less than kine joke here but it's so lame that I dare not use it lest I lose you.)

Edmund Wilson, the splenetic sage of Talcottville, up near Utica, once said that those of us out in God's country to the west of Syracuse "seemed very low grade. Not even pretty girls, but pale grey-eyed lean ill-built Polish women and the usual thick loutish men. One wonders how these men and women can feel enough mutual attraction even to breed more of their unattractive kind."

Well, we do, though I had to go to California to find a spouse. By the way, if you've ever seen a photo of Edmund Wilson, pot, meet kettle.

I've been asked to speak on "The Empire Versus Our Town." Not Thornton Wilder's play, though it, too, is empire's enemy. I recall several years back when the depressed suicidal unfunny monologist Spalding Gray starred as the Stage Manager in a Lincoln Center revival of *Our Town.* The poster featured an image of the earth as seen from space under the words "our town." Ha ha. Grover's Corners, New Hampshire, is not visible in that photo.

Neither is my town. Or yours. That was the point: It was a universalism divorced from all particularity.

Senator William Fulbright, the only good politician named Bill ever to come from Arkansas, averred that "the price of empire is America's soul and that price is too high." The price can be measured in a thousand and one nonmetaphysical ways, too.

For instance: Twenty-seven years and two months ago, I sat in Rochester's War Memorial Auditorium watching the Wyoming Indians, the smallest basketball-playing school in Section V, contend for the Class D championship. Now, ever since the first point guard dribbled out of the primeval ooze, Wyoming had dwelt in the basketball cellar. The team had never before come close to a sectional title.

What made this game wrenchingly poignant was that it was also Wyoming's swan song. Wyoming High School was to be snuffed three months hence, a victim of onerous state education mandates.

Virtually all of Wyoming fit into one patch of the cavernous War Memorial. There were proud parents, craggy old-timers, little brothers and sisters struck dumb by the size of the arena. Hand-scrawled banners bore such legends as "Wyoming High will never die." But of course it would. The team won a thrilling game; the players and townspeople embraced on the playing floor, sobbing without shame. And then it was over. The following fall, Wyoming High School's fifty-six students would be tuitioned out to neighboring schools. They got those school vouchers that make the dull hearts of Beltway conservatives flutter. So instead of walking to their fine old brick building, which admittedly lacked the state-required complement of computers, they could ride buses for an hour each way.

The consolidation—the murder—of rural schools, and the communities they served, began as a project of progressive educators in the early years of the twentieth century but achieved its most destructive force at the dawn of the Cold War.

We lost many tens of thousands of rural schools during the consolidation craze, which was spurred on by that high priest of Cold War pedagogy, James Bryant Conant, the Harvard University president who had spent the First World War in the chemical warfare service and the Second working on the atom bomb, devising ever more grisly ways of killing people he had never met, before he turned his malevolent attentions upon the nation's schoolchildren. Conant the barbarian, in a series of well-funded and highly publicized reports—front page of *Time* magazine—demanded the closing of all high schools with fewer than 400 students because of the urgency of the threat posed by the Soviet Union. American slackers and their quasi-anarchic system of local education were being outpaced by grim little Ivan Sputnik. Many of these schools were closed, over the passionate objections of parents and the citizens of small communities—I've written about this in my worst-seller, *With Good Intentions?*—though decades later, education researchers found that small high schools of under 400 students seem to get the best results. Alas, it was too late. Many of those small schools were long gone, domestic casualties of the Cold War.

I do like it when the elements of a unified field theory align. Years ago I spent a morning with Joe Paterno, Penn State football coach. (I saw nothing, I assure you.) I asked Coach Paterno why the once-sterling quality of high school football in the Western Pennsylvania coal country had deteriorated in recent years. He looked at me and said, "School consolidation."

Thank you, Joe!

The peremptory demands of empire alter our lives in ways both gross and subtle, seemingly innocuous and malign. Daylight saving time, which used to be called "war time," was a World War One innovation that eventually became permanent; henceforth, the time of day was whatever we said it was—sun be damned. The metric system, which is permeating American life despite widespread opposition from ordinary people—which is to say, people who do not matter in American politics—is a project primarily of that unholy alliance of big science, big business, and big government, which coalesced during the Cold War. We have been hectored for five decades now to cut off our feet and submit to the meter. As though with the snap of a finger—the crack of a whip—the empire can make people adopt an entirely new system of measurement.

(When our daughter was in school, we told her to miss questions about metric measurements on purpose. To hell with the liter. Then again, we also told her to insist that Pluto was a planet. That explains those lousy science grades. . . .)

"It's up to you not to heed the call-up. . . ."

I could borrow from Edwin Starr and title my remarks "War: What is it good for?" But then you'd fear that you were in for a cold shower of sanctimony, annoying and cloying like those "War is not healthy for children and other living things" bumper stickers that could drive Mother Teresa to want to napalm a nursery of Vietnamese babies. (That went too far, Bill.)

War is good for some things. Prosthetic limb manufacturers. The moving van industry. Funeral parlors located near military bases. It is also, in my favorite hunchback Randolph Bourne's aphorism, the health of the state: the essence and engine of big government. Shredding liberties, feeding young men and now young women into the charnel house.

Stephen Crane, of *Red Badge of Courage* fame, said that the unacknowledged part of war was "the great country back of the line of fight—the waiting women, the lightless windows, the tables set for three instead of five." The home front. This is the side of war that is most real for ordinary Americans yet which seldom interests our politicians or even our artists—except for singular patriots like Harold Frederic or Michael Cimino.

War and a militarized state efface and pervert everything that traditionalist conservatives profess. War forcibly uproots people; it alters courtship patterns; it spreads venereal disease, if not democracy; it separates husbands from wives and parents from children; and it always leads to a spike in the divorce rate among service personnel—because while absence may make the heart grow fonder, love's truest expression is fixity. And war consigns the offspring of soldiers to government daycare—in fact such daycare was the spawn of war, born as the Lanham Act of 1940, which subsidized over 3,000 daycare centers to incarcerate Rosie the Riveter's neglected kids. (You know, I hate all that Rosie the Riveter crap, as if women working ten-hour days in a bomb factory making weapons of mass destruction while their children are tended by government employees in daycare camps was a quantum leap forward for womankind. Down with Rosie the Riveter; up with Dorothy Day!)

The army today is the biggest single daycare provider in the land of the semifree: over 200,000 American tykes are being raised in military daycare centers, seven days a week, 365 days a year, in what the Pentagon, with its usual tone deafness to Orwellian rings, calls "the total army family."

No agency of the federal government has done as much to subvert the American family as has the Department of Defense. For sheer obscenity, it's hard to beat separating mothers from children, then sending those mothers across the world to assist in the taking of life.

At church services, or public gatherings in my town, a prayer for our young neighbors in the armed services will usually end with "Bring them home safely." I never have the heart to tell folks that the architects of US foreign policy do not intend for these soldiers to come home en masse—*ever*. They will be over there—from Europe to the Middle East—forever. It's no coincidence that the slogan most reviled by the foreign policy establishment—after "America First," of course—was "Come home, America," the patriot George McGovern's beautiful, even poetic plea in 1972. Because America ain't ever supposed to come home.

Yet McGovern's call resonates still. Opinion polls show little enthusiasm for the rash of US interventions on the other side of the globe. This is the "isolationism" that haunts the bloodless dreams of the war makers. An isolationist, as far as I can tell, is someone who wants neither to kill nor be killed by foreigners.

In the mid-1950s the largest public works project in American history, the National System of Interstate and *Defense* Highways, was sold as a national defense measure, just as was the first large-scale federal intervention in American education, the National *Defense* Education Act of 1958. The interstate would scar our lovely country, bisect and trisect and destroy countless city neighborhoods, encourage the scattering of the population, and serve as a massive subsidy to the trucking industry and to chain stores, thus warring on small town Main Streets. It was a federal government project that changed American life in many ways. Yet the creation of the National System of Interstate and Defense Highways was never discussed in the pages of *National Review*, flagship publication of the Cold War Right. Because the Right had lost sight of America. It became obsessed with communism, and so this very un-American ideology of anticommunism came to dominate the Right. The Warsaw Pact mattered—Warsaw, New York, and Warsaw, Illinois, did not.

But of course the interstate, like the space program and Beyonce, is a symbol of American greatness. (No man is without his petty hypocrisies; I drove largely on the interstate to get here.)

I love and often quote G. K. Chesterton's line that a "patriot never under any circumstances boasts of the largeness of his country, but always, and of necessity, boasts of the smallness of it."

It's not a hard-and-fast rule but the launchers of and propagandists for American wars and American Empire have tended to be men without local loyalties, little loyalties, men who would never think to boast of the smallness of their country.

USA! USA!? Uh-uh. More like Ever Batavia. Sweet Home Alabama. Straight Outta Compton. Fourth of July, Asbury Park.

Lincoln Colcord, the Maine novelist, saw his country losing itself as it stood astride the globe. If America was everywhere, then it would be nowhere. To Colcord, home was Searsport, Maine, and his encomium upon it might stand as the creed of the whole Little American tradition: "It's not a bad place, much like many others, but the secret of our love for it lies in . . . [this]—we know it intimately. This is the lesson I get from Thoreau. Love your own pond. All are beautiful. Be contented where you are. Content!—a lost word in our America. This restless ambition—I cannot feel the truth of it. I cannot follow there."

Lacking "restless ambition." Loving your own pond. Being content. What a stark contrast to the reigning idea of "success" in America. Those who stay loyal to their little postage stamps of ground are said to be losers; to abandon it, to trash it, to forget it—that's the freeway to American success. We are expected to look away, to prize the distant over the near-at-hand, to care more about Hollywood than Hudson, or Baghdad more than our own backyards.

So what is to be done?

Booker T. Washington said cast down your buckets where you are. Which is what, as I understand, the Bruderhof have done here in the aptly named Walden.

The late novelist Norman Mailer, who said that he was to the left of the liberals and to the right of the conservatives—wisdom's place!—diagnosed the modern malady: "The style of New York life has shifted since the Second World War (along with the rest of American cities) from a scene of local neighborhoods and personalities to a large dull impersonal style of life which deadens us with its architecture, its highways, its abstract welfare, and its bureaucratic reflex to look for government solutions which come into the city from without (and do not work). . . . Our authority has been handed over to the federal power. We expect our economic solutions, our habitats, yes, even our entertainments, to derive from that remote abstract power, remote as the other end of a television tube. We are like wards in an orphan asylum. The shaping of the style of our lives is removed from us—we pay for huge military adventures and social experiments so separated from our direct control that we do not even know where to begin to look to criticize the lack of our power to criticize. . . . [O]ur condition is spiritless. We wait for abstract impersonal powers to save us, we despise the abstractness of those powers, we loathe ourselves for our own apathy."

The cure is a revival of local life, of self-government, of citizenship. Mailer himself pointed the way home in one of the few truly creative and sensible political campaigns of the imperial age: his 1969 candidacy for mayor of New York City, which was based in love and loyalty, essential motives of any decent movement. Mailer wanted New York City to break off and form the fifty-first state, and then he wanted to devolve almost all power within the new state to the neighborhoods of the five boroughs, which would also be free to secede, correcting the mistake of 1898: that is, Brooklyn's absorption into the soulless blob known as the City of Greater New York. The adjective *greater*, in referring to political entities, means in practice "lesser."

Now, the word *secession* sets off alarms at the thought police station, because a previous secession was largely for the ignoble purpose of protecting slavery, but the principle itself is as American as sandlot baseball, hard cider, and runaway slaves. (For more on this you might consult my book *Bye Bye, Miss American Empire*, a history of American secessions.)

Mailer called for "a hip coalition of the left and right," for everything from "black power to Irish self-righteousness." "I'm running against urban renewal," he exclaimed, in Jane Jacobsian language, which is to say he was on the side of beauty, poetry, sentiment, history . . . losers. His secondary plans—for instance, holding a world series of stickball to be played in the lanes of Wall Street—shone with a luster that not even his running mate for city council president, Jimmy Breslin, could appreciate. (Breslin did get off one of the campaign's best lines, however, when after election day he said, "I am mortified to have taken part in a process that required bars to be closed.")

Mailer's campaign was not an amusingly picturesque sidelight but was, rather, part of a rich tradition of American dissent, of visions of alternative

Americas, that runs through the Anti-Federalists, the Loco Focos, the populists, the distributists and Catholic Workers, the Old Right, the prairie power participatory democracy wing of the New Left, and it is in this room today, and in this place.

Peace. Place. They belong together.

Thanks for listening.

38

The Tolling of the Bell

On the Bicentennial of the First Presbyterian Church of Elba

Two hundred years and counting. Photo by Lucine Kauffman.

How thoughtful of the founders of this church 200 years ago to have timed this bicentennial to coincide with a Bills bye week.

Lucine and I moved to Elba thirty years ago this fall. Which means of course we're still new people. When you're new to a town or a church you feel like you're walking into a movie halfway through. You don't know the characters' backgrounds, you don't know why so and so doesn't like such and such . . . and you learn quickly that you'd better not speak a critical word about anyone because you're probably talking to the guy's cousin.

Actually, an elderly relative who was into genealogy told us a few years ago that in fact I do have ancestors who lived in Elba in the 1880s and 1890s. One of those ancestors showed up in what passed for the police blotter of that day for stealing horses. So we've never claimed him.

When Lucine and I and our then infant daughter Gretel started attending this church in the mid-1990s, we felt welcomed, immediately, unreservedly. This was a house of neighborliness and love, and "love thy neighbor" is among the most beautiful teachings of Christianity.

It's been a long time. Heck, I remember when Matt Braddock was a boy preacher.

This month marks the bicentennial of the organization of what was known in 1822 as the First Congregational Church of Elba. The names of its pioneer members are on the document gracing the wall in the narthex. The first church on this site seems to have been built in 1829 or 1830; it was extensively renovated in 1867, the same year this congregation became Presbyterian. The original church burned to the ground in 1874, and this building in which today we gather together was erected in 1875.

In their lively account of the church's history, Agnes and Frances Graham wrote of the 1874 fire that "the Presbyterian church and the hotel on the four corners were entirely destroyed. Some wit remarked that the fire extended from heaven to hell." Sadly, a later tavern on the four corners, the Stumblin' Inn, was consumed by fire just a couple of years ago; unlike that apparent den of iniquity of the nineteenth-century, the Stumblin' Inn was a place of community and sodality.

For a church to endure 200 years—that's one-tenth the history of Christianity. Very impressive.

One of the hallways in the Elba school is lined with photos of graduating classes going back to the 1920s. I always get a kick out of looking at those pictures. Some of the names and faces recur every generation; only the hairstyles change. I think this gives kids, even those whose families are new to Elba, a sense of continuity, of belonging, of being part of something bigger than just themselves.

I had the same feeling reading through accounts of this church's history by various Grahams and Wilfords and Jean Price: members now deceased but with familiar, even comforting, names.

For two centuries the people who make up this church have persevered, in prosperous times and in depression, in peace and in war, in eras of good feelings and in years of strife. Certain themes run through all those years: for instance, fellowship.

Dinners, socials, clubs—Elba Presbyterians have seized on any excuse for getting together, enjoying each other's company. For years there was an annual Washington tea, at which two distinguished-looking congregants would dress up as George and Martha Washington. Lucine and I were speculating on which of today's Presbyterians might play George and Martha. (I won't tell you whom we chose.)

There seems always to have been a sense of fun, of sly humor, in this church, too. I associate this strain with Stew and Jean Hare, whom we used to sit behind. At the end of each service they'd turn around and make some witty remark—especially if one of the hymns exceeded four verses, which was Mr. Hare's limit. Maybe Tom's, too.

In that good-humored spirit, Chester Wilford, who was before my time, though no doubt many of you remember him, turned a wry eye and pen to his account of the pastors this church has had over the years.

You have to read between the lines, which is where the good stuff often is.

Mr. Wilford tells us of such pastors of the past as the Reverend J. R. Walbridge, who was "a bit ahead of his time in Elba." After six months in the pulpit in 1937, Reverend Walbridge "left for new fields," says Chester Wilford. "Those who knew him well were sorry to see him go." The rest . . . not so much.

The Reverend Louis Lunardini, who shepherded this church in the mid-1960s, was "a great sermonizer and humorist," according to Chester Wilford, "but [he] prided himself on doing little work." Not really the best way to ingratiate yourself with a farming community.

There's also a reference to the son of the Reverend Earl Davis. Mr. Wilford expresses the hope that the boy will "refute the old image of the minister's son." I was not familiar with that particular stereotype; I'm sure our own Johnny Tipton does not live down to it.

The longest serving pastor of this church was the Reverend Gabriel Corwin, who presided from 1841 to 1867. The other day I left a penny on his stone in the Maple Lawn Cemetery. Barbara Tipton has only eleven years to go to pass the good Reverend Corwin.

Beautiful music has long filled this church. The Graham ladies record that in the early twentieth century the Reverend Farley Porter opened each service with the hymn "safely thru another week," a title that does not exactly resound with confidence. C'mon, Farley, cheer up. As the great farmer-writer Wendell Berry says, be optimistic . . . even though you have considered all the facts.

It is said that during the early years of the twentieth century, Elbans for miles around set their clocks every Sunday to the tolling of the church bells at 10, 10:30, and 11 a.m., and 7 and 7:30 p.m.

Chester Wilford, who must have been a poetic old codger, ends his history of the First Presbyterian Church with the sentence, "so the work of the church goes on in Elba, and the same bell was tolled Christmas Eve last."

May the bells of the good news continue to ring out, with joy and love, and may we always set our internal clocks to the timeless truths taught, preached, and sung within this blessed church.*

---

*This homily was delivered by a Roman Catholic.

39

Where at Least a Few People Know Your Name

2023

"He can buy a bottle and drink at home."
"It's not the same."

—"A Clean, Well-Lighted Place," Ernest Hemingway

After the fire. Courtesy of *The Batavian*. Photo by Howard Owens.

Let us now praise famous bars. Well, famous in that they kindle a warm nostalgic glow in my sentimental gut.

The Fieldhouse, Batavia, NY
McVan's, Buffalo, NY
930 Club, Washington, DC
Eddie Van Cleve's Sportsman's Lounge, Santa Barbara, CA
O'Lacy's, Batavia, NY
The Stumblin' Inn, Elba, NY

Here's one thing about a life lived locally: coming face to face and living cheek by jowl with one's landsmen makes them impossible to idealize. Lord Acton said that exile is the nursery of nationalism, but Hoyt Axton, as if speaking for my town, said, "The whole darned world is going to pot / You might as well like it cause I'm all that you've got."

As a nineteen-year-old hick intensely homesick for Batavia (though I was domiciled just thirty miles away at the University of Rochester), I came home all the time, but in our nocturnal bar-hopping my buddy Chuck and I (who had cut our hair short, like the kids in far-off places I read about in *New York Rocker* and *New Musical Express*) gagged and groaned over the corporate-prole musical tastes of our Batavia coevals. REO Speedwagon? Just shoot me!

Chuck and I would sing along with the angry young man Graham Parker—"Don't bother with the local girls"—as we made the hour-long drive to McVan's, the dive at the end of downscale Hertel Avenue, and the only Buffalo bar welcoming punk and new wave bands in 1979.

(Not bothering with the local girls is easy when the local girls won't bother with you. I had to go to Los Angeles to find my wife, so maybe old Graham was right.)

Sometimes we'd bring our friend Mick, a Jimmy Connors lookalike from a long line of Irish tipplers. But Mick joined the army and later moved south, working in a Tyson plant and fighting off the family curse. His older brother Frankie stuck around town. A few years back Frankie drunkenly fell down the steps of a local watering hole and helped pay his medical bills by holding a fundraiser at the same bar. That's my kinda Go Fund Me!

Chuck and I once endeavored to drink every beer in the cooler of that bar (which we will call Shea's), a feat that a slender gent named Moose still calls to my attention. I am not glorifying overconsumption of alcohol, a stupid and destructive act, but as Willie Nelson sings, "There's nothin' I can do about it now."

(May I interrupt this stagger down memory lane for a political note? Under the ancient American practice of federalism, each state once set its own minimum age for alcohol purchases. In New York it was a civilized eighteen. Until 1985, when the Reagan administration and Transportation Secretary Elizabeth "Liddy" Dole bullied the fifty states—under penalty of withheld funds—into submitting to a uniform nationwide drinking age of twenty-one. Secretary Dole was the ferinely ambitious trophy wife of powerful Senator Bob Dole, the Kansas Republican who had dumped his frumpy first wife for the plastic sorority girl Liddy. Bob Dole is best known to later generations for his televised pitches for boner medicine—not exactly an advertisement for Liddy, eh? When the senator ran for president in 1996, he carried a copy of the US Constitution as a prop. I assume his flunkies had scissored out the Tenth Amendment.)

Sorry for the parenthetical spleen. As an Anti-Federalist I have a soft spot for federalism.

A coupla years back, the custodian at my wife Lucine's place of employ, who tended bar at Shea's Friday nights, dared her to drop by.

"If I do, will you make me a vodka tonic?" she asked.

"No," replied Jim, with the same bluntness he evinced as a classmate of mine at BHS. "No tonic. Order beer."

So we stopped at Shea's of a Friday evening. Lucine surveyed, with amusement, the wall décor: yellowing, corners-ripped '70s pinups—nothing so predictable as Cheryl Tiegs or Farrah Fawcett-Majors, more like the third-string Snap-On Tool Girl. *Pace* Hemingway, Shea's isn't exactly clean or well-lit, but then that's not Scott and Zelda in the corner, either.

Lucine sauntered up to the bar.

"Whaddaya want?" growled Jim.

"Vodka with lime."

"No limes."

Lucine pulled a lime from her purse and placed it on the bar.

"Don't have a knife."

She pulled a knife from her purse and proceeded to slice the lime.

The regulars at the bar hooted. One observed that this was the first fruit or vegetable ever seen in Shea's. Lucine did a tequila shot with my old friend Billy and all was well.

Today, I don't know anyone from McVan's or the late '70s Buffalo punk scene. Hell, I didn't then, really, any more than I'd know a soul were I to lollop into La Scala tonight. But I do know a few of the boys at Shea's and can fall into easy conversation with them, having shared a place and a portion of communal memory for several decades.

If Shea's had a jukebox it'd be blaring Bachman Turner Overdrive instead of John Cale or the Circle Jerks, but as my late and wryly weary Armenian father-in-law used to say in his cultured Syrian-Cypriot accent, "What are you going to do?"

Anonymity has its advantages—were I in need of a prescription for some embarrassing rash or disease I'd rather it be filled at a generic out-of-town Rite-Aid than at a local pharmacy—but there is no feeling quite like that of belonging.

Five summers ago, Lucine and I watched on a Sunday morning as the Stumblin' Inn, which had served as the tavern in the center of the little village of Elba for a century and a half, burned to the ground. I don't believe the cause of the fire was ever determined.

The Stumblin' Inn's owner-operators were the brothers Stork and Jim. Stork, the mayor of Elba, was a hulking shaggy-haired ex-Marine who resembled Ted "Mad Stork" Hendricks, the wildman linebacker of the Oakland Raiders. Jim was his Iggy Pop–thin brother. A centenarian would say they looked like Mutt and Jeff.

The Stumblin' Inn was one of the only truly multigenerational bars I've ever known. Patrons ranged from twenty-something Katelyns to eighty-something Earls. Like a good neighbor, Stork looked out for Elba's daughters when, invariably, they celebrated their twenty-first birthdays at the Stumblin'.

Stork and Jim and much of the community stood vigil that Sabbath morning as the (uninsured) gray-painted wooden structure collapsed into rubble and dust, despite the best efforts of the volunteer firefighters. Some of those who bore witness were hushed and somber; others told stories of their first legal drink, a first date, inebriated hijinks.

Stork and Jim have passed on. They died of natural causes, though surely a broken heart counts as a comorbidity. Grass grows in the vacant lot where once sodality was seeded. Every Halloween season mourners put up playful effigies of Stork and Jim, with painted pumpkins bearing the Neil Young lyric "Hey hey, my my, Rock & Roll Can Never Die."

Even teetotalers are moved by the sight.

40

There Is Always Baseball in Batavia

It Was the Summer of '68, 2019

Bill and Mike Kauffman of the Lions Club Cubs. Photo by Sandra Kauffman.

I grew up one block south of Dwyer Stadium and MacArthur Park. (When I was a kid I thought that the wonderfully bombastic Jimmy Webb song about leaving the cake out in the rain was about our neighborhood park.) I started going to Batavia Trojans games with my parents and brother in the Summer of Love, 1968. I was eight years old. I hadn't liked baseball before this because I'd been stung by a bee on a ballfield and associated the sport with pain—little did I know!—but that summer I became hooked. We sat behind the Trojans dugout, which used to be on the first-base side. Why Batavia's teams spent thirty-plus years looking into the sun I do not know, but sometime in the 1970s they switched sides. (No need to open the old first-base bleachers versus third-base bleachers debate here, eh?)

In that summer of '68 we four Kauffmans sat most every game with a motley crew that included three pretty teenaged girls named Sharon, Karen, and George (yes, George was a female, I'm sure of it), and an older LeRoy couple (older: hell, they were probably younger then than I am today!) who pounded down the Gennys and rallied the crowd with lusty cries of "We Want a Hit!"

In my memory, which is given to exaggeration and fabulism, the team was a juggernaut, but thanks to the dubious wonders of the internet I see that in fact they finished under .500, as most Batavia teams do. No matter. They had a fiery manager, Bob "Dusty" Dustal, who gave the poor umpires unshirted grief. I remember the slugging catcher, Mike Murray, who hit a robust .341 but never made it beyond AA, and the ambidextrous outfielder Tom Breving, who used to buy lemonade at our stand at the corner of Bank and Douglas as he walked to the games. Another catcher, Dave Bike, came up and sat with us one game after he'd been tossed for arguing with the ump. On the last day of the season he gave my brother an uncracked bat.

As a boy, the players were the thing, but the older I got the more I realized that the charm, the allure, the magic of minor league baseball is the fans, the friendships, the communal aspect of the gathering. There are people at the games whose names I do not know and yet in a very real sense I know them, I know their faces, and because Dwyer Stadium is calibrated on a human scale each and every man or woman, boy or girl, is essential and if absent would be missed. G. K. Chesterton wrote about a "democracy of the dead," and those who have passed on are a presence at Dwyer. They're in my mind's eye. Heck, I still owe Bill Dougherty a beer, and though I may not pay him off till the next life—assuming that the polka classic "In Heaven There Is No Beer" is a lie—I half expect to hear his laugh every time I walk through the gates.

I wouldn't attend a major league game if you gave me a free ticket, but except for the years I lived away, Dwyer Stadium has been a second home for me, and the people in the stands and players on the field have enriched my life in ways they cannot begin to know.

Bottom of the Ninth

2018

> The question is not really why things end;
> The question is are endings merely endings,
> Or beginnings also?
>
> —Jesse Wills, "Requiem for a Church Condemned"

The Nashville Fugitive poet's question hangs over our heads this summer like a waterlogged baseball suspended in midair. For the Batavia Muckdogs (nee Clippers, then Trojans) of the Class A New York–Penn League, born 1939, are no longer under local ownership.

We were one of the last truly community-owned teams—an arrangement hated by professional leagues in all sports and levels. A twenty-five-person volunteer board ran the franchise, which was bequeathed us by our baseball-loving and civic-minded forebears.

As the longtime vice president of the board, my duties consisted mostly of watching baseball games and hoping fervently that president Brian Paris didn't die. We both held up our ends of the bargain.

I shan't bore you with accounting details, but during the 2007 season we incurred an unusually large, somewhat murky, and certainly unsustainable financial loss. Standing at the abyss, we were rescued by our Burned-Over District neighbors, the Triple A Rochester Red Wings, who for the last decade have managed day-to-day operations while we retained ownership. This past off-season, the league vetoed a continuation of this partnership and seized the franchise, which will play out the string in Batavia until a buyer can be found. (Benevolent millionaires who want to keep the team here are welcome to apply!)

Home away from home. Painting by Patricia Burr/Collection of Bill Kauffman.

Our fate was sealed when the league embarked on a policy of madcap geographic expansion, so that it now stretches from Burlington, Vermont, to Aberdeen, Maryland, and from Staten Island to Morgantown, West Virginia. The result? Eight-hour bus rides, vastly inflated lodging and transportation costs, and the purging of the small cities that once were the heart and soul of the New York–Penn League. Oneonta, Geneva, Jamestown, Elmira, and Niagara Falls are gone; Auburn and Batavia are the last of the Mohicans. What shall it profit a league if it gains Norwich, Connecticut, but loses its soul?

Growth, as Ed Abbey used to say, is the ideology of the cancer cell. And of professional sports.

Our board had no choice but to approve the forfeiture. Nevertheless, I cast a symbolic Nay vote on behalf of seventy-nine years of Batavia baseball supporters.

"This going to end up in a book?" asked Dr. Al Barcomb, the last Montreal Expos fan.

I suppose it just might.

But for now, I gotta keep my mouth shut.

In any event, Dwyer Stadium will never be empty. It has too many ghosts. If and when the league flees its birthplace, we will play host to a team in one of those amateur circuits for collegians who have yet to turn pro.

Batavia is a damn good baseball town. Before the bottom dropped out last summer, average per game attendance for the Muckdogs was about 6 percent of the city's population, which placed us, on a per capita basis, in the top half of the league. Yes, Brooklyn outdraws us by seven to one—but Brooklyn also has a population more than 175 times larger than ours. We apologize for nothing.

And if I may play George Babbitt for a moment, Batavia is the smallest city in America with both a professional baseball team *and* our own symphony orchestra. So there.

The Muckdogs had consistent support from small businesses, the mom-and-pop shops and delis that are the lifeblood of any community. The big-box chain stores and corporate welfare clients, by contrast, wouldn't even buy an outfield sign. The bastards.

Ah, but on to more pleasant baseball thoughts.

Three summers ago, I sat in the backyard under a summer sun reading "Mr. Hunter's Grave," a lovely Joseph Mitchell profile of an African American sexton in a Staten Island cemetery. Upon finishing, I walked in the house and declared to Lucine, "We've never been to Staten Island. Let's just go."

Checking my emails, I found a note from Richard Kostelanetz, the avant-garde litterateur, with whom I had last corresponded perhaps twenty years earlier.

"Comrade Bill," he asked, "will you accompany the Muckdogs" when they travel to play the Staten Island Yankees?

The coincidence so staggered me that I had to take a walk to regain my sense of balance. Surely this was providential! Or was it a sinister trick by some gremlin in the cursed computer, luring us to a capsizing Staten Island Ferry?

We didn't go. It's an eight-hour trip to the Whitehall Terminal. But maybe this summer, Kosti. Maybe this summer.

Maybe Everything that Dies Someday Comes Back

2021

For years I was vice president of the Batavia Muckdogs, one of the only community-owned teams in professional baseball. (There is no ownership

Muckdogs win the pennant! Photo by Mike Janes.

setup more roundly detested by profit-minded speculators in pro sports.) We teetered on the financial ledge, the poor sister of the New York–Penn League, and it wore on us. Sometimes during a game I would stare at one of the faithful—maybe Alice, a lifelong fan whose bandana covered a head balded by cancer treatments; or Mark, a retarded older man whose imagination, like mine, was coterminous with Dwyer Stadium's boundaries—and think how crushed he or she would be if we lost our team.

As it happens, we lost Alice and Mark before we lost the team, but this past offseason the dead souls who run Major League Baseball (MLB), and who believe that sentiment and history are for losers, terminated the New York–Penn League. They just up and killed it as part of a bloodbath that reduced the number of minor-league baseball teams from 160 to 120. Even those surviving six score franchises are grim visaged today, for minor league baseball as a quasi-independent entity has been abolished, and its relicts are locked into the fetid antechambers of MLB.

A circuit that was born in Batavia in 1939 (as the PONY—Pennsylvania–Ontario–New York—League) died in Manhattan's oppressive Time-Life Building, apt headquarters of Major League Baseball, during the winter of COVID-19.

The chief executioner, I regret to say, is a native Upstate New Yorker named Rob Manfred, MLB commissioner, who announced the slaughter using words like "modernizing," "prioritized," and "unrivaled technology"—the argot of an android destroying what it does not understand.

As if pulling the plug on forty teams and their host communities weren't enough, Major League Baseball also renamed the remaining leagues. It's as if a dull-witted 1970s East German bureaucrat had been named Commissar of Nomenclature. So the International League, founded in 1884—the cleverly monikered Trenton Trentonians won its first championship—is now denominated Triple-A East. The teams of the storied Sally (South Atlantic) League have been parceled out to High-A East and Low-A East. The Pacific Coast League, pride and joy of prewar California baseball, is now Triple-A West.

What sort of automaton thinks that these generic handles are superior to historic appellations? Wouldn't even the most cynical and sleazy Madison Avenue image-meister urge the retention of the old and fabled names, if only as a nostalgia-soaked marketing ploy?

Well, to hell with them. Because you know what? The Batavia Muckdogs are the men they couldn't hang. We have resurfaced in the sillily named but fine-quality Perfect Game Collegiate Baseball League, an amateur summer division for college ballplayers who are considered potential pro prospects.

We're no longer community-owned, but the new proprietors hail from Elmira, New York, hometown of Mark Twain's wife Livy. This is a good sign, since reports of our death, like Twain's, were greatly exaggerated.

Unlike the pros, the PGCBL encourages teams to sign a local lad or two. The reborn Muckdogs will include the son of a fellow I used to play ball with and also the grandson of friends.

I detect faint but discernable echoes of the town baseball leagues that flourished into the 1940s, with their fierce place-based rivalries. This spirit endures in modified form at the high school level, although the consolidation of school districts into multitown agglomerations dulled the edges and muted the passions.

Enraged as I was by Manfred's massacre of the minors, I'm starting to think that ours was a promotion by demotion.

For what is true in life is true in baseball is true in politics. Localize. Decentralize. Break down the overly large into a smaller and more human scale. I mourn the death of the minors but perhaps it presages the death of the majors, or at least the rebirth of baseball in organized forms that respect the local, the idiosyncratic, the unregimented.

I'm here to tell you that there is life after major league–affiliated baseball, just as there will be life after the welcome and deserved collapse of the American Empire.

The 2021 Muckdogs begin their season in late May. I'll be there in the third-base bleachers, surrounded by friends and family and the ghosts of all those—like Alice and Mark—who have hallowed these grounds. Hey hey, my my, / Real baseball can never die.

On Finding Myself a Character in a Baseball Book

2025

I highly recommend *Homestand*, Will Bardenwerper's new book contrasting the community-enhancing qualities of grassroots baseball with the soulless corporate product that Major League Baseball has become—and it's not just because I am a central character therein. The book is at once a beautiful portrait of bleacher-level society and a scathingly effective indictment of the automatons who are destroying the American game.

Will spent the summer of 2022 in and around Dwyer Stadium, home of the Batavia Muckdogs, an independent team of college ballplayers. This

Small Ball Is Best. Photo by Will Bardenwerper.

amateur ball club was the feisty successor to professional teams that had graced our fair city since 1939. Alas—or should I say enragingly—Major League Baseball exterminated 40 of the then 160 professional minor-league teams in the COVID winter of 2021 with all the sensitivity of an obnoxious drunk squishing a cockroach.

Will and I became great friends that summer. I figured I'd be quoted here and there in the book, but I show up so much that my brother emailed me, "I'm twenty pages in and already tired of you." I can imagine a querulous reader, after exposure to my occasional pronouncements, grumbling, "Jeez this guy has a lot of opinions. Doesn't he ever shut up?" Or as Neil Young sang, "Is there anything he knows that he ain't said?"

Betsey Higgins and Ginny Wagner, best friends who make the forty-five-minute drive from Buffalo every game because they love the atmosphere and both the comedic and dramatis personae in the stands, are also featured prominently in *Homestand*.

Given that Will Bardenwerper's first book, *The Prisoner in His Palace*, a layered and thought-provoking account of the dozen young American servicemen who guarded Saddam Hussein in the final months of the Iraqi tyrant's life, is currently in preproduction, the Buffalo gals are casting an envisioned *Homestand* movie.

Betsey has Cate Blanchett as herself, while Ginny has floated Queen Latifah and Da'Vine Joy Randolph to impersonate her. In a fit of madness or kindness they suggested Kevin Costner play me, but they later dialed that back to Michael Shannon. Hey, it's better than the ghosts of Ernest Borgnine or Marty Feldman.

I kid Betsey and Ginny that come June and a new baseball season, visitors to Dwyer's third-base bleachers will be monitoring their behavior and measuring it against the characterizations in the book. And who knows where that will lead, as the late Pat Conroy found out.

Conroy's novel *The Great Santini* was based on his relationship with his brutal and pitiless father, a Marine pilot and truly miserable martinet. *The Great Santini* was filmed to great effect with Robert Duvall in the lead role. Who does not love Robert Duvall? The actor suffused the irredeemable prick Santini with a gruff and amusing humanity. Author Conroy reported, to his astonishment, that after the hit movie made his father famous, the old bastard softened considerably, modeling himself after Duvall's portrayal. Life was imitating art which had imitated life.

However, this is not always replicable. After one of my books featured my wife Lucine as a (thoroughly and accurately!) praiseworthy figure, I sometimes asked her, "Why can't you be more like that character in the book?" I can report that this line of inquiry does not work.

Homestand has gotten deservedly laudatory notices, and endorsements by sluggers ranging from Robert (*Bowling Alone*) Putnam to Ron (*Bull Durham*) Shelton, but Will says that his one dispiriting if instructive revelation has been that "many in the traditional 'baseball media' are afraid to touch this book—I suspect out of fear of being seen as too critical of MLB and losing access or otherwise facing adverse professional consequences."

It's rather like reporters for *Pravda* or *Izvestia*, circa 1970, declining to interview Aleksandr Solzhenitsyn. Sure, he'd make for a lively chat, but a guy's gotta think of his livelihood, after all. Mustn't take all this reporter jazz too seriously.

I hadn't realized that MLB commissioner Rob Manfred (an Upstate New York native, to my embarrassment) was quite so sensitive to criticism—or so vindictive. Ron Shelton does say of the man who killed the professional Muckdogs and thirty-nine other teams in small or unfashionable or hardscrabble cities, "Manfred is the Antichrist—and you can quote me on that!" Harsh, maybe, but Ron is right!

When the sports-writing guild has descended to the point where its ink-stained wretches—I mean inhalers of keyboard dust—won't call the Antichrist the Antichrist, we're a long way from Red Smith and Jim Murray, baby.

Homestand is, by my reckoning, the most anti-MLB but pro-sandlot and hick-circuit baseball book ever published. Strike a blow for the true American game and read it.

Index

About the Author

Bill Kauffman is the author of a dozen books, among them *Dispatches from the Muckdog Gazette*, which won the 2003 national "Sense of Place" award from Writers & Books; *Look Homeward, America*, which the American Library Association named one of the best books of 2006 and which won the Andrew Eiseman Writers Award from the University of Rochester; and *Ain't My America*, which Senator George McGovern called "one of the best books I've read in years." He also wrote the screenplay for the 2013 feature film *Copperhead*.

His writings on subjects from baseball to political history have appeared in numerous publications, including the *Wall Street Journal*, the *Los Angeles Times Book Review*, and *The American Scholar*. He is a columnist for *The Spectator* and *The American Conservative*, and a founding editor of Front Porch Republic.

Bill has worked as a magazine and book editor and as a legislative assistant to Senator Daniel Patrick Moynihan. He lives in his native Batavia, New York, with his wife, Lucine.

www.ingramcontent.com/pod-product-compliance
Lightning Source LLC
LaVergne TN
LVHW090601070826
845179LV00020B/101